Bball basics for *Kids*
Basketball Handbook

Coach Bobby Kaplan

bballbasics.net   bballbasics@aol.com

Bball Basics for Kids
A Basketball Handbook

iUniverse books may be ordered through booksellers or by contacting:

iUniverse
1663 Liberty Drive
Bloomington, IN 47403
www.iuniverse.com
1-800-Authors (1-800-288-4677)

ISBN: 978-1-4620-4373-6 (sc)
ISBN: 978-1-4620-4371-2 (e)

Library of Congress Control Number: 2012914545

Printed in the United States of America

iUniverse rev. date: 8/7/2012

Bball basics

is dedicated to all the volunteer coaches who work so hard for our children ... you know who you are ... I salute you!

What Kids Say about Bball basics

- *Bball basics* is fun and easy to read. I practiced the drills and got a lot better.

- The boys in my class could not believe it—after practicing the shooting drills, I made more foul shots than they did!

- I kinda knew how to play basketball already, but *Bball basics* raised my game to a new level.

- I made my eighth-grade team with the help of *Bball basics*.

- The pictures in the book are of kids just like me—not actors or pro stars—I liked that!

- Stretching before a game gets me ready to play. The stretching pictures in *Bball basics* helped a lot.

- My brother and I read *Bball basics* together. It was good to have someone to practice with.

- HOOPS is so cute. He was fun and made the game easier to learn.

- My friend and I are on the same team. We taught our teammates the *Bball basics* way of shooting—and we all got better.

- I feel real good about myself—I practiced the *Bball basics* dribbling drills and could now dribble well with both hands.

- I can't believe that my picture is in a real book! I'm so happy that my coach customized *Bball basics* for my team.

- I can sure dribble all over ... thanks to *Bball basics*.

Why I wrote this book

A friend of mine asked me to recommend a basic basketball book for his nine-year-old grandson. I said, "Give me a day or so to do some research."

I went online and found numerous books supposedly covering basketball fundamentals for kids. However, most books on the market were targeted to the more mature teenage audience—not for a child just learning how to play the game.

I chose a few potential books geared for the beginner and delved a little deeper into the material covered. I was disappointed with both their content and their presentation. They were either infantile in their approach or so complex that an experienced basketball coach would have a hard time understanding what they were saying.

I then remembered that in 1994, when I was the owner/director of a sleep-away basketball camp, I produced a basic basketball handbook that I gave out to campers attending my summer camp. I rummaged through my stored boxes and found a copy. I reviewed my handbook and concluded that it would be a good beginners' book. I gave it to my friend who then presented it to his grandson.

A few days later, my friend, who is very knowledgeable about the game, told me that his grandson loved the book so much that he even took it to bed with him, falling asleep while reading it.

I gave the handbook to others with kids and received similar reviews. Many people suggested and encouraged me to publish my handbook.

After many rewrites and additions Bball basics took shape.

Bball basics presents a step-by-step, easy-to-read, fun way to teach the fundamentals of the game of basketball.

Enjoy! Bobby Kaplan

Customize Bball basics for your Basketball Program

All coaches, administrators, principals, camp directors, youth organizations, parents, etc., will be very excited by this special feature—this book can be personalized for you!

I have designed Bball basics with a unique feature: You can customize and reproduce this book with your players' pictures substituted for the pictures included in this book. In addition to the pictures, you can further personalize the contents by adding a page describing your particular program, and it will be placed at the beginning of your book.

Details of this unique feature can be found in the back of the book (page 117).

Hi, Kids,

It's not hard to learn to play the game of basketball, the most popular game in the world, and it can be lots of fun.

Bball basics is a step-by-step, easy-to-read book showing how to learn the most important skills of basketball, such as dribbling, passing, shooting, rebounding, and playing defense.

Bball basics will also tell you how to warm up correctly and eat right, give you a brief and interesting history of this great game, share some inspirational stories and provide a glossary (a list) of basketball words so you know what they mean.

My friend **Hoops** will be helping me explain how to play this game. If you pay attention, try hard, and practice the right way, you can be a good player.

Hi. I'm **Hoops**. I'll be helping Coach K teach you the basics of the game of basketball.

We are going to have so much fun while we learn.

So listen up, try hard, and remember: it's up to you how good you want to be.

You can do it!

Bball basics CONTENTS

CHAPTER 1 Getting Started in Bball

Let's go!

Basketball is a fast-moving game played by over five hundred million people all over the world. Basketball combines your individual skills—how well you play—with the skills of your teammates. All members of the team must work together for one common goal. On **offense**, when your team has the ball, means doing everything together to help score baskets. On **defense**, when the other team has the ball, means doing everything together to stop the opposing team from scoring.

Basketball may seem like a hard game to learn, but like most games, the more you play, the easier it is to understand what's going on.

I'm sure you have watched games on TV and seen coaches quickly draw squiggly lines showing where players should go and what players should do. You may ask yourself, "How does anyone understand what the coach is telling his players? This seems so hard to understand." You will see ... **It is not!**

Actually, basketball is a simple game. If you try hard and practice the right way, your basketball skills will improve. How much they will improve depends on you and the effort you put into getting better.

Hi, Guys. Bball basics will help you become a good player.

I'll bet that if you learn the game with the help of this book, you will soon be drawing squiggly lines showing your teammates where to go and what to do on the court.

It took some time, but I tried hard, and now I'm a Bballer!

'Hoops'

22

1

Playing sports should be fun. If you are interested in becoming a basketball player just for the fun of it or to join a team, Bball basics will give you the solid beginner-level skills needed to play this sport.

You will not become a good basketball player overnight. Take your time learning, but learn it the right way. Improvement will come if you want it to happen.

One way to help you reach your goal of becoming a basketball player is to **get a friend** to work along with you. Together you can read this book, understand what it is trying to teach you, practice what it says to do, and coach each other to improve your individual skills.

One word about **equipment**: In the beginning, don't use a ball too big for your hands or practice shooting on a basket too high for you. Get a smaller basketball, lower the rim, and practice the right way. As you get older and stronger, you can work your way up to a regular-sized ball and a rim ten feet off the ground.

The Basics of the Game

The goal or aim of the game is to score more points than your opponent, the player or team you are playing against. Scoring happens when you put the ball through the basket. Baskets count for different points depending on where you shoot from. Some baskets count for three points (those taken from behind the three-point line), some for two (shots made in front of the three-point line), and some for one point (baskets made from the free-throw line).

Players move up the court by passing the ball to a teammate or dribbling (bouncing) the ball up the court. While five players make up a team in a real game, you can play the game of basketball with fewer players, even one against one. You can certainly practice most skills by yourself.

How This Great Game Started

The game of basketball was invented by a gym teacher named **Dr. James A. Naismith** back in the winter of 1891 in Springfield, Massachusetts. He invented the game so that kids at his school could run around indoors playing a game during the cold, snowy winter months.

Dr. Naismith tried different ideas before he attached a peach basket to the gym wall ten feet off the ground. Students were divided into two teams. The team that put the ball (which at that time was a soccer ball) into the basket more often won the game.

At first, after each basket scored, a ladder had to be brought out to take the ball out of the basket. This slowed down the game until Dr. Naismith came up with the idea of drilling a hole in the bottom of the peach basket so that a rod or stick could be used to push the ball out of the basket. Eventually, the bottom of the peach basket was cut out so that the ball could drop easily through after a basket was scored.

Dr. James A. Naismith

Over the next few years the game of basketball grew in popularity, and everybody started to play. Dr. Naismith soon realized that you can't just run around and do what you want—**rules** on how to play the game had to be created.

He developed **thirteen basic rules** for all to follow, and many of these regulations are still followed in today's game. In fact, Dr. Naismith's original regulations regarding the height of the basket, ten feet off the ground, and the diameter of the basket or rim, eighteen inches wide, are still used today.

The First Basketball Court

Rims and nets were soon substituted for the peach basket, and the basic rules of the game were accepted and widely used. The first backboard, which was made of wood, was introduced in 1904, not to help shoot the ball but to stop fans from interfering with the shot! Many gyms had a running track as the balcony, and fans watching the game would swat at the ball to stop it from going in!

No one is sure how the painted rectangle got on the backboard, but it became known as the **shooter's square**, helping shooters get the correct angle to "bank," or shoot the ball off the backboard.

It was not until 1901 that players could bounce (**dribble**) the ball, but only one bounce was allowed. **Dribbling** did not exist until that point! The original soccer balls that were used were too heavy to bounce. In 1909, **dribbling** as we know it today was introduced—you can now bounce the ball as many times as you want. Dribbling became an offensive skill.

A Basketball Court around 1920.
Notice the "rocking chair" on the left.

4

A Basketball Used in the 1920s. The laces and the outer seams made this ball hard to dribble.

Since the ball was still heavy and had laces on the outside, it took crazy bounces, making dribbling difficult. As the sport grew and grew in popularity, more and more rules were made to improve the game. Improvements were also made with the basketball itself. In the 1950s the ball was fixed to resemble the ball we use today, and dribbling became an offensive weapon.

Girls' basketball had a somewhat different beginning or evolution from the boys' game. At first, boys were not permitted in the gym to watch a girls' game because boys and girls did not mix socially during the early years of the sport in the 1900's. The girls' game of basketball was a lot different from the boys'. The girls' court was divided into zones (areas), and the players could not move out of their zone. Strange! Eventually, two rovers were permitted; only those players were allowed to move around the whole court. It was not until 1971 that women's basketball rules were changed to allow all players to use the full court.

Dr. Naismith could never have imagined that his newly invented game to get students running around in the winter months would become one of the most popular sports in the world.

Women's Basketball around 1900. Notice that the net is not open on the bottom. A stick had to be used to push the ball out of the basket.

Important Dates in Basketball History

1896: First college basketball game is played between Stanford University and the University of California

1936: Basketball becomes an Olympic sport

1938: The first college tournament is held (called the NIT, the National Invitational Tournament)

1939: The NCAA (National Collegiate Athletic Association) tournament is created

1946: The first professional basketball league is formed, called the Basketball Association of America (BAA)

1949: The NBA (National Basketball Association) is started, replacing the BAA

1954: The NBA institutes the twenty-four-second clock (meaning that the offensive team has to shoot the ball within twenty-four seconds)

1967: Another professional league is formed called the ABA (American Basketball Association). It combined with the NBA in 1976.

1972: Title IX Legislation is passed by Congress providing women with the same sports opportunities as men

1979: The NBA adopts the three-point shot (a basket made from behind the three-point line is worth three points)

1980: The shot clock is introduced in the college game along with the three-point line

1997: The WNBA (Women's National Basketball Association) is formed

6

The Basketball Court: Where It All Happens

Basketball is played on a court with two baskets (hoops) on opposite ends of the court.

Although there are official dimensions (sizes) for both junior high and high school basketball courts, often courts do differ in length and width. What is always the same is that there is a foul line and a three-point line, and the size of the basketball rim is standard at eighteen inches in diameter from one side of the rim to the other side.

The picture below shows the official high school basketball court with some important dimensions (eighty-four feet long and fifty feet wide) and areas on the court you need to know about. The official junior high school court is similar, but the dimensions are seventy-four feet long and forty-two feet wide. College and professional courts are bigger and have different dimensions for many areas.

As you know, basketball is an international sport and is played all around the world. Basketball courts outside the United States are a little different from those in America. Over the next ten years, the international basketball courts will be changing to look like those in the United States. This will help make the game the same around the world.

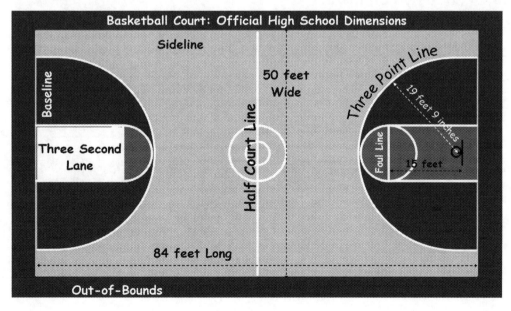

7

Here are some basic areas on a basketball court that you need to know about.

- **In bounds:** The area inside the court lines (the gray area in the picture). The long side of the rectangle is called the **sideline,** and the shorter side the **baseline.**

- **Out of bounds:** The area outside the court lines

- **Foul line:** The line from where you shoot foul shots or free throws. Each foul shot made is worth one point.

- **Three-point line:** If you shoot behind this line, the basket is worth three points. Baskets made inside the three-point line are worth two points.

- **Three-second lane:** The white area near the basket in the picture of the court. If your team has the ball, you cannot be in this area for more than three seconds at a time.

The Ball and Basket

A regulation-sized **boys'** basketball is 29.5 inches in circumference (which means around the whole ball). The diameter (from one side to the other through the middle) of a boys' ball is less than 9 1/2 inches.

A **girls'** basketball is slightly smaller. A regulation girls' basketball is 28.5 inches in circumference and is just over 9 inches in diameter.

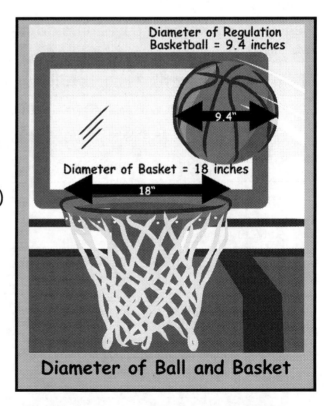

Diameter of Regulation Basketball = 9.4 inches

9.4"

Diameter of Basket = 18 inches

18"

Diameter of Ball and Basket

If you remember, when the game of basketball was invented in 1891, the game was played with a soccer ball. It was not until the mid-1900s that a new orange-colored basketball, similar to the one used today, was introduced. The ball was orange so that it would be easily visible to the players.

Kids, would you believe it ...

Two basketballs can almost fit into the basket at the same time!

The basket, or *rim*, is a lot bigger than you think.

How Long is a Game?

For elementary, middle school, high school, and professional leagues, a game is divided into four parts or quarters. A quarter in a high school game is eight minutes long. In younger grade levels it may be anywhere from six to eight minutes long. In professional games quarters are twelve minutes long. College games are divided into two halves, each twenty minutes long.

BASIC BASKETBALL RULES and VIOLATIONS

Most games have rules. These rules or instructions tell you what you can and can't do to play the game right.

Basketball also has rules to follow. When you break these rules it's called a **violation,** a fancy word for breaking a rule. When you play a game, a **referee** (usually wearing a funny black-and-white striped shirt) makes sure that you are following or obeying the rules.

Many of the rules and regulations of the game may seem at first to be hard to understand or confusing. But the more you play the game, the better you will understand what is okay to do and what not to do.

Let's go over some of the basic basketball rule violations.

What is a foul?

Basketball is a physical game. Players are moving around a lot and do bump into and hit each other. However, you cannot bump or hit an opposing player in such a way that it hinders (stops) his ability to play offense or defense. Whether you mean to do it or not, it is still a foul. The best way to explain this is to give you some examples. You cannot:

- Hold a player going for the ball

- Slap the arm of a player shooting the ball

- Trip a player running down the court

- Jump on someone's back as he or she goes up for a rebound

- Charge into a player who is standing still on the court

How many fouls are you allowed?

In middle school and high school, a player is allowed up to **five fouls** in a game. After committing the fifth foul, the player has **fouled out** and must leave the game and is not allowed to return. So although everyone gets fouls called against them—it is a part of the game—you have to be careful not to foul too much. Your team needs you in the game! Also, if you foul someone, the other team will get possession of the ball (meaning they are now on **offense** and you are on **defense**). If you foul a player shooting the ball, or your team has too many fouls, they may be rewarded and shoot one or two foul shots.

What is traveling or walking?

When you are holding the basketball you cannot travel or walk with it. You are allowed to pick up and move one foot off the floor, but your other foot, called the **pivot foot**, must stay on the floor. You can turn your pivot foot in any direction, but you cannot pick it up off the floor.

You cannot take steps with the ball without dribbling it. This is called a **traveling** or **walking** violation, and when it is called the other team gets possession of the ball.

What is a double dribble?

If you are moving and dribbling the ball and stop dribbling, you cannot dribble again. If you do dribble again, it is called a **double-dribble** violation.

A **double-dribble** violation also happens when you dribble the ball with two hands at the same time. You are only allowed to dribble with one hand at a time. You can switch hands while dribbling—first dribbling with your right hand and then switching your dribble to the left hand—but you cannot dribble with both hands at the same time.

A **double-dribble** violation results in possession of the ball going to the other team.

11

When is the ball out of bounds?

Basketball is played on a rectangular court with lines around the edges. Inside the lines is **in bounds**, meaning where the game is played. Outside the lines is **out of bounds**, meaning if the ball is hit or thrown outside the lines of the court, the ball is **out of bounds** (off the court). The ball is then given to the other team to **in-bound** it—throw the ball into the court to a teammate to continue playing.

What is a three-second violation?

An offensive player, a player whose team has the ball, cannot stand in this lane near the basket (see page 7), for more than three seconds at a time. This lane is called the **three-second lane**. If the referee sees you "hanging out" in the three-second lane too long, he will blow his whistle and call you for a **three-second violation**. The other team will then get possession of the ball.

IMPORTANT PEOPLE ON A TEAM

I'm the **coach,** the leader of the team. I help improve the basketball skills of each of my players and then put them together to form a team.

I teach the team offensive and defensive skills and plays to help them have fun together as a team.

I like to win games, but more important than winning is making sure my team plays the right way—showing **sportsmanship!**

Coach K will talk about sportsmanship very soon. Now let's introduce the team.

Let's Meet the Players

In a game, five players are on the court at the same time for each team. **Hoops** is going to help me explain what each position is about and what they are usually expected to do. Coach K sometimes calls these positions "spots," and they are numbered one to five.

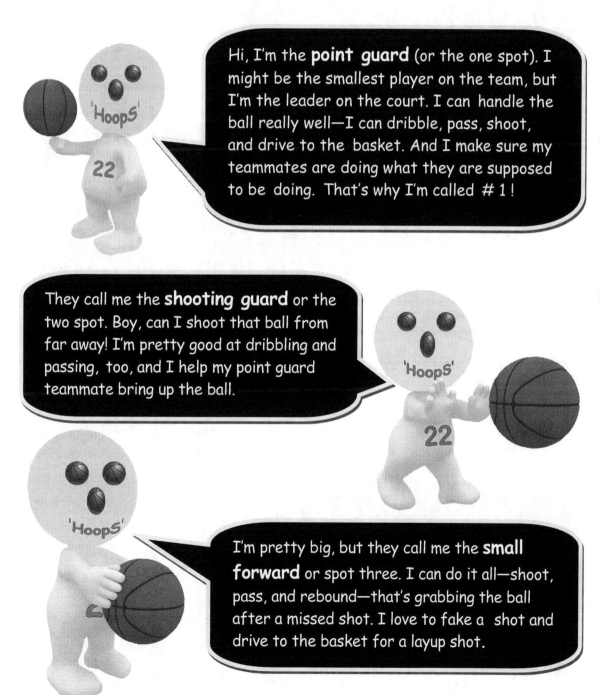

Hi, I'm the **point guard** (or the one spot). I might be the smallest player on the team, but I'm the leader on the court. I can handle the ball really well—I can dribble, pass, shoot, and drive to the basket. And I make sure my teammates are doing what they are supposed to be doing. That's why I'm called #1!

They call me the **shooting guard** or the two spot. Boy, can I shoot that ball from far away! I'm pretty good at dribbling and passing, too, and I help my point guard teammate bring up the ball.

I'm pretty big, but they call me the **small forward** or spot three. I can do it all—shoot, pass, and rebound—that's grabbing the ball after a missed shot. I love to fake a shot and drive to the basket for a layup shot.

Power forward, that's who I am. I'm big and I'm strong and Coach K calls me the four spot. I usually shoot near the basket and love to rebound and start a fast break with a good outlet pass—that means rebound, turn, and pass the ball up-court to my buddy the point guard.

I'm the biggest player on this team. The five spot ... the **center.** I love fighting for rebounds, especially offensive rebounds. I often get fouled, so I need to be a good foul shooter. I usually play with my back to the basket, get the ball, make some quick moves, and hit a layup shot.

I'm the **manager** of this team. I may not get a "spot" number, but I am a very important person. Without me, the game won't be played. I keep the score and the time and make sure the players have enough water to drink.

Some Thoughts on Sportsmanship

Sportsmanship can be summed up in one word: **respect**.

Respect your teammates, your coach, the referee, the opposing team, and the fans watching the game. Play the game with effort, observe the rules at all times, and win or lose courteously—in a nice way.

Your opponent in basketball is not your enemy. You don't have to like someone to be respectful. For example, you may not agree with a referee's call, but you have to respect the call. You can question the call, but do so in the right way—with respect.

Refereeing a game is a tough job. Without a doubt, during the course of a game there will be some calls made by the referee that may not seem right or accurate. You must remember that a ref must make decisions in a split second—very quickly. No one is perfect! You must accept the call and play on. As you grow as a player, try refereeing any sport, and you will see how difficult it is.

Basketball is a physical sport—meaning that players often bump into each other, get hit with an elbow, trip or fall on the court, and so on. However, during a game you cannot intentionally hit, push, kick, or trip the other team's players. Even if you do not do it on purpose, the referee can call a foul on you.

Trash talking—making fun of or talking "down" to people—has no place on the court. Trash talking can lead to rough physical play and, in some cases, actual fights. Just play the game as best you can without embarrassing the opposing team, coaches, fans, referees, or your own teammates. Be a good sport!

Sportsmanship includes respecting all, being sensitive to others, following the rules, complimenting the good plays of your teammates and even your opponents, congratulating the winner, encouraging and cheering your teammates, helping less-skilled teammates to get better, not embarrassing anyone, and accepting blame when it is deserved.

And most importantly, grow and learn from criticism—like a coach giving you ideas on how to be a better ballplayer. Become a champion player and person both on and off the court!

Remember *You can win a game and be a loser, and you can lose a game and be a winner. Be a good sport and have fun and you will always be a winner.*

CHAPTER 2 BALL HANDLING

The ball and you are one

Ball handling is the most important part of becoming a good basketball player. Ball handling, simply put, is **becoming good friends with your basketball. The ball becomes part of you.**

There are four basic parts to ball handling: **dribbling, the triple-threat position, passing,** and **ball-handling skills.** Let's cover dribbling first.

DRIBBLING

Dribbling can be a powerful offensive tool (what to do when you have the ball) if used correctly.

You should start your dribble from a **triple-threat position.** This is a certain way to stand when you dribble, pass, or shoot (we will cover this very soon). But remember, once you start your dribble, your choices are limited—

1: Dribbling Position ... Protecting the Ball.

once you stop you cannot dribble again. You should not dribble without good reason. Always have a purpose. You should dribble to:

- Get yourself into a position to score

- Get the ball to a place where you can set your teammate up to score or pass

- Get yourself away from the defense (the player guarding you) and protect the ball

How to Dribble

#2: On the Move … Body Low … Dribble Low

- Bounce the ball with one hand.

- As you bounce the ball, spread your fingers wider and wider. This will help you control the ball better.

- Use your lower arm (forearm), wrist, and fingertips to dribble the ball. Your palm should not be hitting the ball

- Keep your dribble below your waist. If you dribble too high, the defender, the person guarding you, can steal the ball. Don't bounce up and down with your body as you dribble

- Keep your dribbling hand close to your body. This protects the ball so a defender will have a hard time stealing it. If you keep your elbow far from your body, a defender will be able to reach in and steal the ball

- Keep your chin up so you can see the court. Don't look down.

- Stay on the balls of your feet (which means toward your toes). This will give you balance, and you will be able to move more quickly

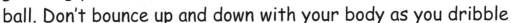

IMPORTANT *You must be able to dribble well with both hands. If you are right-handed, practice dribbling twice as much with your **left** hand. If you're a lefty, dribble twice as long with your **right** hand.*

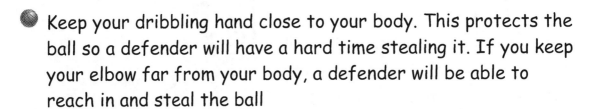

18

DRIBBLING: Fun Ways to Practice

Dribbling takes practice. Practice dribbling for just ten minutes a day for three months and you will become a good dribbler.

First, find a flat area to practice dribbling and spend ten minutes straight dribbling—four minutes with your strong hand and then six minutes with your weak hand. Second, start dribbling with one finger (your index finger); then add more fingers as you get better and better.

After a while, start dribbling while walking. As you get better at dribbling you can start running—switching hands while you dribble. Once you have mastered the basics of dribbling, you can try the **"stop and go"** dribble at different speeds (dribble slow and then stop moving your feet but keep dribbling; dribble fast and then stop moving but keep dribbling).

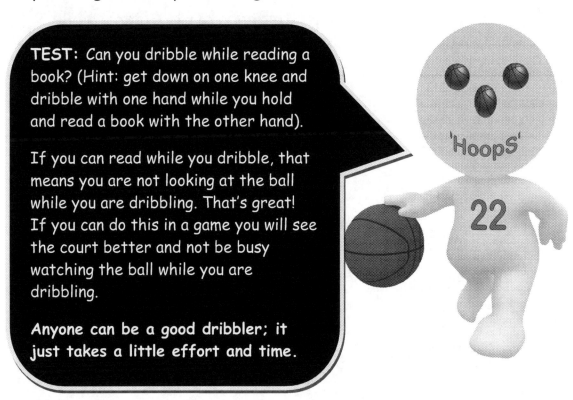

TEST: Can you dribble while reading a book? (Hint: get down on one knee and dribble with one hand while you hold and read a book with the other hand).

If you can read while you dribble, that means you are not looking at the ball while you are dribbling. That's great! If you can do this in a game you will see the court better and not be busy watching the ball while you are dribbling.

Anyone can be a good dribbler; it just takes a little effort and time.

'Hoops'

22

Some More Fun Dribbling Drills

Chair Dribble Drill: Sit on a chair (watching a sports movie like *Hoosiers*) and dribble. Make sure to switch hands and dribble more with your weak hand.

Between-the-Legs Dribble Drill: Learning how to dribble between your legs is a good skill that improves ball handling. But only use it in a game when there is a purpose to such a dribble—like when you are closely guarded and you want to switch your dribbling hand. **Don't use it to show off!**

3: Chair Drill

With your feet spread wide facing forward and your body low to the ground, bounce the ball from one hand to the other between your legs. Start slowly so you get the hang of it. After a while, begin to lift your head and not look at the ball. Increase the speed of your dribble and begin to move forward as you dribble.

4: Dribble Between the Legs

5: Don't Look at the Ball

Stopping the Ball Stealers:
Protecting the Ball While Dribbling

If you don't want someone to steal the ball, you've got to protect it.

The best way to protect the ball is with your body. Your body should always be between the defender (the person guarding you) and the ball.

 # 6: Ball to Side, Head Up, Arm Out

How to Protect the Ball

If the defender is on your left, dribble the ball with your right hand and have the left side of your body facing him.

It is very important to learn how to dribble **with both hands** so that you can protect the ball no matter where the defender comes from.

Even if the defender is right in front of you, you can still protect the ball by turning your body sideways and dribbling the ball with your hand furthest from the defender.

When you make this shift, the defender must either foul you (by pushing, holding, or hitting you) or go around you in order to steal the ball.

 # 7: Body Protecting the Ball

'HoopS'

22

It's *cool* to dribble well.

You can do some fancy stuff with the ball. But remember— don't show off! Dribble to help you score, pass to a teammate, or get out of trouble.

Let's review some important dribbling skills.

Dribbling

- Dribble with your body in the triple-threat position.

- Dribble for a purpose.

- Look up, not at the ball.

- Use your fingertips for good control.

- Dribble below your waist.

- Dribble close to your body.

- Protect the ball with your body.

- Practice dribbling with both hands.

8: Dribbling Position

THE TRIPLE-THREAT POSITION

The **triple-threat position** is one of the most important stances—the way you position your body—in basketball. The triple-threat position puts your body in **balance**—ready for action.

Let me explain this **balance** thing. I can't think of any sport where you are playing standing straight up. You are always crouching down, which helps you to move quickly and be in balance.

Try this "experiment." Get a friend to stand straight up. Put your hands on his shoulders and give a push—he will move backward. Now have your friend bend his knees. Give him a push again. Bet you he does not move backward that much! Why? Because he was in better **balance**!

You should use the triple-threat position on both **offense** and **defense**. When you're in this position, you're ready to do the following on **offense**:

- Pass or catch a pass
- Dribble
- Shoot

On defense, the triple-threat position is often called the **defensive stance**. How you position your body on defense is almost the same as offense.

When you're in this position, you're ready to do the following on **defense**:

- Guard the man with the ball
- Guard a man who doesn't have the ball

9: Triple-Threat Position

How to Stand in the Triple-Threat Position

- Place your feet shoulder width apart.

- Your shoulders should be **squared up**—facing the basket.

- Bend your knees.

- Put your weight on the balls of your feet.

- Your heels should be just slightly touching the floor.

- Don't hunch over too much. Try to keep your back straight.

- Keep your hands above your waist.

10: Triple-Threat Position

- Keep your head up—see the action around you.

Remember *Practice the triple-threat position until it becomes automatic—you can do it without thinking. You'll know you've mastered it when you're playing in a game and you suddenly realize ...*

"Hey I'm standing in the triple-threat position and I didn't even try to do it!"

PASSING

Basketball is a team sport, and a good passer is a tremendous help to the team. Good passing leads to baskets, but bad passing leads to turnovers (giving the ball back to the other team).

11: Chest Pass

As you become a better shooter, you will realize how important it is for you and your teammates to pass correctly. A good pass helps the shooter get into a comfortable shooting position. In addition, if you want to receive a pass, always give the passer a target, hand or hands out, protected by your body.

You must be careful not to let the opposing team know where you might be passing the ball. This is called **telegraphing your pass**. If you let a defender know where you are going to make the next pass, he may step in between the pass and your teammate and then steal the ball. A smart way to avoid telegraphing your passes is to fake a pass in one direction and pass in another.

The two basic types of passes are the **chest pass** and the **bounce pass**.

A **chest pass** is when you throw the ball with two hands to a teammate without the pass touching the floor.

A **bounce pass** is when you throw the ball with two hands to a teammate and it bounces.

'Hoops'

22

25

THE CHEST PASS

A **chest pass** is usually used to pass around the perimeter (the outside areas) of the court. A **chest pass** moves faster than a bounce pass.

How to Throw a Chest Pass

\# 12: Ball Grip

- Pass in the **triple-threat position**.

- Spread your fingertips on the ball on both sides. Don't hold (grip) the ball too tightly.

- Keep the ball lower than your chin and step into your pass—toward your target. Aim at your teammate's chest.

\# 13: Step into Pass

- When you release the ball, snap your wrists so that your palms face down and your thumbs point down. This will put some backspin on the ball, which makes the pass more accurate and faster.

- Remember that it's your job to throw a pass your teammate can catch.

- Don't throw a high pass to a really short person.

\# 14: Wrists Snap ... Thumbs Down

- Don't throw a really hard pass to a teammate not strong enough to catch it.

26

THE BOUNCE PASS

The **bounce pass** is used when it is not possible to pass directly to your teammate with a chest pass. If a defender is guarding your teammate tightly (very close), it may be better to throw a bounce pass.

The bounce pass is usually used to pass inside the perimeter (toward the basket). You can use a bounce pass to pass under the hands of a defender. This is called passing **in traffic**.

How to Throw a Bounce Pass

\# 15: The Bounce Pass

- Set up as you did for the chest pass, in the **triple-threat position.**

- Aim to bounce the ball two-thirds of the distance between you and your teammate.

- Proper backspin will make the ball jump softly off the ground and into your teammate's hands, so remember to snap your wrists when you pass the ball.

- Your teammate should give a target (hands out) to receive the ball waist high.

- A bounce pass is easier to catch than a chest pass.

Important *Once you have mastered the art of passing, you can start faking some passes, which means making believe you are going to throw a pass. To do this, just go through the regular movements to throw a pass but don't release the ball.*

27

Catching a Chest or Bounce Pass

The most important thing to do when **catching a pass** is to get full control of it (making sure you are holding the ball firmly) before your next move.

- Never take your eyes off the ball as it gets passed into your hands.

- Keep your hands up with your fingers spread open, giving a target for the pass.

- If the ball is thrown to the right side of your body, catch it with your right hand extended (toward the pass) more than your left hand. If the ball is thrown to the left side of your body, catch it with your left hand extended.

- After catching a pass, protect the ball by tucking it in close to the side of your body in the **triple-threat position.**

16: Target … Hands Open, Up, and Ready

17: Catch and Tuck in Triple-Threat Position

BALL-HANDLING SKILLS

Simply put, **ball handling** is getting to know your basketball. The basketball should become part of you. Know how it feels, what it weighs, and how it bounces! Keep in mind the importance of controlling the ball equally well with both hands.

There are many drills to improve your ball-handling skills. Here are a few basic ones that will give you a good feel for the ball, are fun to do, and will give you confidence (a feeling that you can do it) on the court.

Get really good with these drills and soon you will be able to come up with your own drills to improve your **ball handling**.

Remember to use only your fingertips to control the ball, and, eventually, don't look at the ball when you are doing these drills.

Passing Drill: Simply pass the ball from one hand to another in front of your body. Next, try the same thing but behind your body. Then, do both of these while you are walking and running.

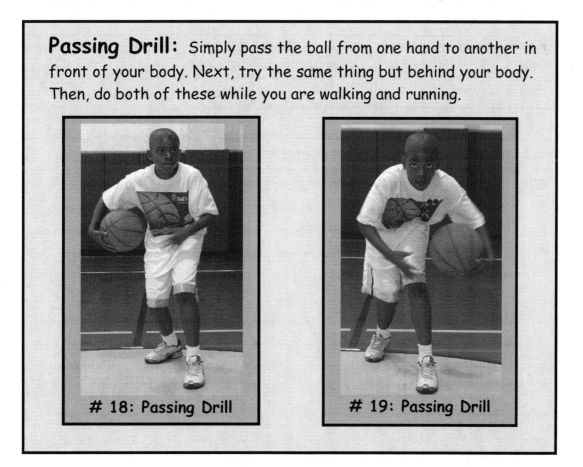

18: Passing Drill

19: Passing Drill

Circle Drill: Circle the ball around your waist by passing it from one hand to the other. Make sure to switch directions every so often ... go faster and faster. Next, in a **triple-threat position**, move the ball around your right leg and then your left. Go faster and faster.
Next do the same thing around both legs in a **figure eight (8)** direction.

20: Circle Drill

21: Circle Drill

Tap Drill: Hold the ball above your head and begin to tap the ball from one hand to the other using your fingertips. Once you get good at this, begin to tap the ball lower and lower toward the floor.
You know you are getting really good at ballhandling when you can start tapping above your head....move down to the floor and then back up again.

22: Tap Drill

23: Tap Drill

30

Let's have fun ...
and learn something
at the same time!

I know what you want to do to help your *ball-handling skills*. You want to spin the ball on your finger.

Why not—it will help you get to know the ball better. Just don't do it in a game!

Start by holding the basketball in the palm of your hand with your fingers pointed up. Spin the ball and catch it. Do this a number of times. Spin the ball faster and faster.

The next step is to spin the ball, and while it is up in the air, put the tip of your index finger under it while it is spinning. Keep trying—it takes practice. Before you know it you will be able to spin the ball on your finger while walking around.

Once you have mastered spinning the ball on your strong hand, try doing it with your weak hand. Now you know you are a good *ballhandler!*

24: "I can do it!"

CHAPTER 3 SHOOTING
Expect to make the shot

Shooting is an important part of the game. Sure, you can be a good basketball player without being a good shooter. But to be a well-rounded, complete player you must learn to shoot well.

Shooting is the easiest basketball skill to learn. When you practice the right way, you can become a good shooter. If you really practice hard, you can become a shooting machine!

Once you learn how to shoot well, your mental attitude (how you feel) while shooting will not be "I **hope** the ball goes in" but rather "I **expect** the ball to go in."

Before we learn how to shoot the basic shots in basketball, like an outside shot or a layup, we must keep in mind one important thing: **Do not begin to learn shooting from the three-point line (about twenty feet away).** Begin your practicing of an outside shot five to seven feet from the basket.

Once you master shooting at a closer distance you can then step back a little and practice some more. In a reasonable period of time you will reach the three-point line and **expect** to make the shot, not **hope and pray** that it goes in.

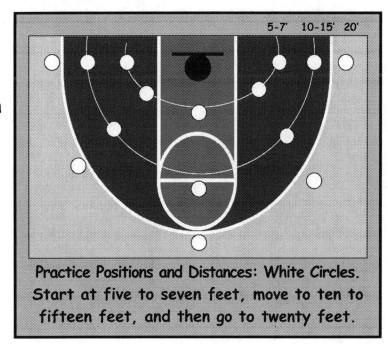

Practice Positions and Distances: White Circles. Start at five to seven feet, move to ten to fifteen feet, and then go to twenty feet.

33

How to Shoot

There are basics you need to practice in order to become a good shooter. You can use these fundamentals for **regular (set) shots, free throws (foul shots),** and **jump shots.**

Many people think they are good shooters, but they can't tell you exactly what they do (the mechanics, the form) to make their shots. It is important for you to know exactly what each part of your body is supposed to be doing while you're shooting. By knowing this, you'll be able to correct your shooting form if you're not hitting your shots. Remember:

● Every part of your body affects your shot

● You must position every part of your body in the right place

When you first start practicing shooting correctly, you may feel awkward (not comfortable). Just give this new way a chance for a week. Soon you'll get used to shooting with the new form and you'll be hitting more shots. You'll also become more confident (feel good) about your shooting ability.

25: Flow of Shot: Get Set

26: Flow of Shot: Release

27: Flow of Shot: Follow-Through

How to become a shooting "Machine"

There are four fundamental steps to learn to become a good shooter: **B** balance, **P** pointy finger, **F** flip, and **F** follow-through. Let's abbreviate them to **BPFF** so we can remember these skills.

B of BPFF Balance

Positioning Your Feet and Body: The Triple-Threat Position

28: "B" Body
in Balance

- Both feet should be pointed directly at the hoop. If you are a righty, your big toe on your right foot should be pointed to the middle of the hoop.

- Don't let your left foot point to the side—concentrate on pointing both feet at the hoop. The reason for this is simple: the ball will go in the direction you are facing. If you face the basket, the ball has a better chance to go straight toward the basket.

- Facing your feet toward the basket is also important because it helps you **square your shoulders** to the hoop (which means that the front of your body and shoulders are lined up in the direction of the shot).

- Your right foot should be slightly in front of your left foot (for a righty).

- The front tip of your left foot should reach the middle of your right foot.

- Your feet should be a comfortable distance apart (about one foot).

P of BPFF   Pointy Finger

How you hold the ball is very important as you learn how to shoot well.

Take your **pointy finger** (your index finger, the one closest to your thumb) on your shooting hand and place it right below the **inflation hole** that is in the middle of the basketball. (The inflation hole is where you fill the baskeball up with air.) Spread your fingers over the ball, keeping your **pointy finger** right below the inflation hole. Your **pointy finger** should **point** the ball directly at the basket. The lower palm of your shooting hand should not be touching the ball.

 # 29: "P" Pointy Finger

Your non-shooting hand helps to hold the ball in the right position. Do not use this hand to push the ball forward. Keep this hand on the side of the ball with your thumb spread back toward the middle of the ball.

Let's have some fun and really understand the *pointy finger* thing ...

Stand about ten feet from the basket holding the ball correctly, with your pointy finger right below the inflation hole. Point your finger right in the middle of the basket. Now move your finger (and the ball) one inch either to the right or the left. Since the ball is not pointed at the basket it will not go in!

So, always shoot the ball with the *pointy finger* pointed at the middle of the basket.

'Hoops'

22

Important *Just a word on gripping (holding) the ball. You want to shoot the ball softly but with control so that it has a better chance of going in. This soft touch will come with practice.*

- *Your grip on the ball should not be too tight. Practice finding a comfortable and relaxed grip.*

- *You don't want to hold the ball too loosely either, because a defensive player can slap the ball out of your hands.*

F of BPFF Flip

Now that you are in **balance** and your **pointy finger** is in the middle of the ball, let's talk about flipping the ball. **Flipping** the ball is putting backspin on the ball to help it go straight and soft toward the basket. **Flipping** the ball will also help you hold your shooting arm the right way. Your shooting arm should form an **"L" shape**.

30: "L" Shape
Shooting-Arm Position

31: Upper Palm and
Fingers Touching Ball

Let's learn how to flip the ball the right way...

- Hold the ball with your shooting hand above your shoulder with your non-shooting hand (your helping hand) on the side of the ball helping to keep it steady.

- Next, make sure that the elbow of your shooting hand is tucked in toward your body. This should form an **"L" position** in your shooting arm.

- Bend the wrist of your shooting hand backward so that the ball is resting on your fingertips.

- Shoot the ball off your fingertips about one foot above your head. Snap your wrist down as you shoot. Watch the ball **flip** with a backward rotation (spin). You know that you're flipping the ball properly if you let the ball bounce and it makes a movement to come back to you. Keep trying this until you get that backward flip.

- Keep practicing your **flip**. Before you know it, you'll be flipping the ball without even thinking about it.

Let's see if you can really *flip* the ball well. Once you have learned to flip the ball using both hands, see if you can go onto the next level of *flipping*.

Do everything Coach K said to do above—except now, before shooting the ball, drop your helping hand from the ball. You should be able to balance the ball above your head using only your shooting hand.

Once you are able to balance the ball with one hand, *flip* it and catch it with your shooting hand. Now you're a really good *flipper*.

Try this Flip:

- Lie down on the floor holding the ball in your hand with your palm facing up.

- Using just your shooting hand, flip the ball up about two feet and catch it with your shooting hand. Do it again and again.

- Make sure to watch for the reverse spin on the ball while your wrist snaps down with your pointy finger being in the middle of your **follow-through**.

32: Balance Ball with Your Shooting Hand, Palm up

33: Flip Ball Up, Snap the wrist, and Catch with your Shooting Hand

F of BPFF Follow-Through

We are almost ready to shoot the ball, but first we must talk about the **follow-through** with your shot. Proper **follow-through** is the last key step in learning how to shoot well.

Follow-through is what you do with your body: your arms, your legs, your wrist, and your pointy finger during the shot and after you shoot the ball.

Learn to follow-through the right way ...

- First, stand about five feet from the basket without the ball.

- Go into the triple-threat position (you're in **balance**).

- Make believe you are going to shoot the ball. Have your arm close to your body (**L-shaped**) with your shooting wrist bent back above your shoulder, ready to flip the ball.

34: Follow-Through

- Make sure your **pointy finger** is pointed at the center of the basket.

- Focus on the front of the rim. You must maintain your focus and concentration and keep your eyes on the hoop at all times. **Don't look at the ball as you shoot; look at the hoop!**

- Now shoot the imaginary ball just over the rim of the basket (always shoot a little higher than you think—**up** over the basket and not **at** the basket). Make sure your **pointy finger** goes right through the rim. Hold that pose until the ball goes through the basket. Do not swing your arms. Practice this often. Soon you will feel relaxed and confident about shooting the basketball.

Now you are ready to actually shoot the ball!

Do everything Coach K said before, but now do it with a ball.

Pick a spot five feet from the basket and shoot using only your shooting hand. Don't move from that spot until you make five shots in a row. If you miss a shot, try to understand why. *Were you balanced? Was your pointy finger pointed at the basket? Did you flip the ball correctly? And did you follow through the right way?*

Once you make five shots in a row from one spot, move to four other spots five feet from the basket. After you make five shots in a row from each of these spots, you can move back a few feet. Use your helping hand and do it again. As you move further from the basket, you will realize that the power in your shot comes from your legs and not your arms. Use your arms to guide and aim the ball.

Before you know it, you'll be at the foul line (which is fifteen feet from the backboard) making shot after shot. Only after you become a *shooting machine* should you attempt three-point shots!

Shooting is easy to learn, but it takes time. Remember...

"Perfect practice makes perfect."

FREE THROWS (or FOUL SHOTS)

Free throws win games. They are different from regular outside shots. No one is guarding you, everyone is watching you, and the game clock is not moving. The final score of the game depends on your foul shots.

Free throws can account for 25 percent (one-quarter) of the total points scored in a ballgame. They are often the **clutch** points that decide the outcome of a game.

35: Eyes Focused on Basket

How to Shoot Free Throws

- 🏀 Get right up to the foul line in the **triple-threat position.**

- 🏀 Bounce the ball two or three times—most players do this to help them focus.

- 🏀 Position the ball in your hands correctly (**pointy finger** at basket, fingers spread wide).

- 🏀 Eyes are focused on basket. Aim shot to go right over front rim.

- 🏀 Concentrate. Nothing should occupy your mind except the ball and the basket. Take a deap breath. Use the shooting method we talked about earlier—**BPFF.**

36 Foul Shot

- 🏀 Once you get it right, do the same thing every time—it will become automatic.

Important *A brief word about the arc (the height) of your shot...*

*You must learn to shoot **up** and **over** the front rim of the basket. When you set up to shoot and release the ball, don't throw the ball **at** the basket. Shoot **up** like a **rainbow**. The arc or height of your shot is important; it gives your shot a better chance of going in.*

*The farther out you shoot, the higher the **arc** needed to make the basket.*

Shoot Up Over the Front Rim ... Not at the Basket

'HoopS'

Practice foul shots as if you are in a real game.

Develop your foul shot starting five to ten feet from the basket. Then work your way to the regulation foul line, which is fifteen feet from the backboard.

There is no defense, nothing to worry about.

Bounce the ball the same number of times each time you come to the line.

Don't jump up when you shoot.

Do the same thing every time you get to the line. Repeat the same shooting form each time.

THE JUMP SHOT

Once you have mastered the basic method of how to shoot correctly, we can go on to the next step, a very powerful basketball tool, the **jump shot**. Learn how to shoot the **jump shot** and you will be very tough to guard!

The **jump shot** allows the offensive player to **jump** higher than the defensive player while shooting the ball. When you are first learning the **jump shot**, remember that you don't have to jump high.

The most important skill to learn is to shoot the ball more quickly—with a faster release than a regular shot. Learning the **jump shot** will give you an appreciation (an understanding) of how important your legs are in all types of shooting.

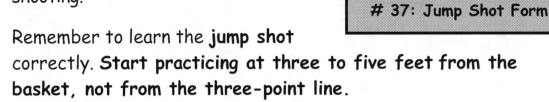

37: Jump Shot Form

Remember to learn the **jump shot** correctly. **Start practicing at three to five feet from the basket, not from the three-point line.**

How to Shoot the Jump Shot

- Start in a **triple-threat position**, five feet from the basket.

- Bring your back foot (left foot for righties, right foot for lefties) alongside your front foot with about a one-foot separation.

44

Using the correct shooting steps talked about before (fingers spread, pointy finger, eyes focused on basket), raise the ball above your head and jump a little (about two inches from the floor). **Flip** the ball at the basket.

Don't worry about making the shot at first. Keep practicing the motions involved. Make sure to follow through in the right way. Before you know it the ball will start to drop into the basket.

Once you get the hang of it, make five jump shots in a row five feet from the basket before moving to another spot five feet farther from the basket. Make the shots and keep practicing farther and farther from the basket.

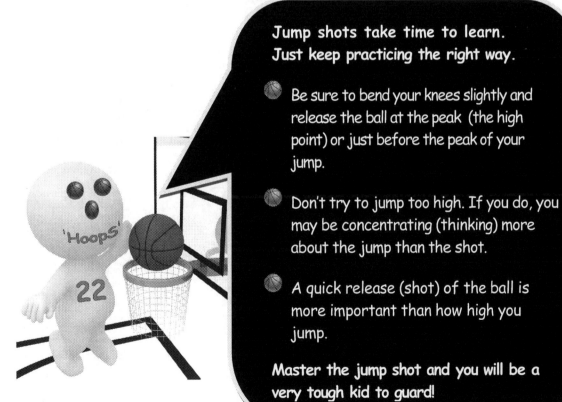

Jump shots take time to learn. Just keep practicing the right way.

Be sure to bend your knees slightly and release the ball at the peak (the high point) or just before the peak of your jump.

Don't try to jump too high. If you do, you may be concentrating (thinking) more about the jump than the shot.

A quick release (shot) of the ball is more important than how high you jump.

Master the jump shot and you will be a very tough kid to guard!

The Layup Shot

A **layup** is a shot at the basket taken while you are running or dribbling to the basket. Most **layup** shots are from either side of the basket or down the middle of the basket.

Most baskets have a rectangle painted on the backboard to help you shoot the **layup** at the correct angle (direction). When done correctly, the **layup** is shot against (off) the backboard and bounces into the basket. The illustration below shows you the correct angles to shoot the ball off the backboard.

Angles for Layup Shot

You must learn how to hit a **layup** from both sides of the basket. When you can do this, you'll be able to make magic happen around the basket. First, learn easy **layups**; then you can go on to more difficult shots like reverse layups, double pumps, cradles, and, of course, the slam dunk.

How to Shoot a Basic Layup

Let's start off with a simple **layup**. I will describe the right way to learn a "righty" layup. "Lefties" should do the opposite.

First, get into a **triple-threat position** about three feet to the right of the basket.

\# 38: Layup Form: release ball softly

- While holding the ball, take a step toward the basket with your **right** foot. Then take a step forward with your **left** foot.

- Jump off your **left** foot with your right foot bent. Shoot the ball off the backboard, hitting the top part of the rectangle on the right side.

- Don't worry about making the shot; that will happen soon enough. Keep practicing: **right, left,** and **up—right, left, and up**. For lefties, from the left side it would be **left, right,** and **up.**

\# 39: Lefty Layup: shoot ball off "shooter's square"

- Hold the ball with both hands as you jump up; then take your **helping** (nonshooting) hand away from the ball and just release the ball softly off the backboard with your shooting hand.

- Once you're comfortable with the footwork, the shots will start to go in. After you make five **layups** in a row from the right, switch to the left side ... **left foot, right foot, and up.** Make ten **layups** with your weak hand.

Now that you can make a layup without dribbling, let's go onto the next level: a running layup. Most layups are made "off" the dribble—you dribble first as you drive to the basket for the layup shot.

- First, start about five to seven feet from the basket. Take one dribble and land in the **triple-threat position.**

- Continue your footwork: **one dribble, right step, left step, and up … shoot.** Get comfortable. Make five **layups** in a row from both the right side and the left side of the basket.

Once you have mastered the one-dribble **layup**, increase your dribble to two and then three dribbles and so on off your fingertips.

As you practice and feel comfortable with your layup shot, remember to…

Jump straight up…landing right before the backboard. Don't look at your feet (their movement should be automatic by now. Keep your eyes focused (looking at) the spot (angle) on the backboard that you have to hit for the ball to go in.

Do not look at the rim of the basket. Focus only on the spot on the backboard.

Relax, just lay the ball off your fingers. Your momentum to the basket creates enough power to shoot.

CHAPTER 4 FOOTWORK BASICS

Dance on the court

Basketball is a game made up of movements: cuts and stops, ball fakes and changing directions. We will cover four of these movements in this chapter: the **jump stop,** the **jab step,** the **ball (shot) fake,** and the **pivot move**.

Proper footwork gets your body to be in the best position on the basketball court. It helps you get a more open shot and make a better pass and puts you in the right position to dribble effectively. Proper footwork will also help you play better defense. Many of these footwork skills make use of the **triple-threat position**, so be sure to remember what we learned about **balance**.

Footwork is very important to becoming a good basketball player. Two simple things you can do to improve your footwork are **jumping rope** and an easy drill called a **line drill, and** both can be done at home.

Jump rope for five minutes a day. While jumping, stop every once in a while and get into a **triple-threat position**.

For the **line drill,** put a piece of tape (two feet long) on the floor. Stand on one side of the line and jump back and forth over the tape. After you get the hang of it, do it faster and faster. Remember to land in *balance*.

The Jump Stop

When you have the ball and are running down the court and decide to stop, you don't want to waste time by slowing down. Instead, you can use a **jump stop**. If you execute a **jump stop** correctly, you can surprise the defense.

40: Dribble and Jump Stop

How to Do a Jump Stop

⚫ While running, decide on a spot on the court where you want to stop. During a game, this can be a split-second decision.

⚫ While running, take a short jump onto the spot you choose. Land on the balls of your feet with both feet hitting the floor at the same time.

⚫ Quickly get into the triple-threat position. You are ready for action (to catch a pass, throw a pass, or take a shot), and you have a choice of **pivot foot** (which foot you can move without a "walking" violation). You can turn your pivot foot in any direction, but you cannot pick it up off the floor.

41: Stop in Balance

⚫ Now do the same thing while you are dribbling. Try dribbling at different speeds. Then do a **jump stop,** and remember to land in **balance**.

The Jab Step

The **jab step** is a fake movement with your feet when you have the ball to help gain some space between you and the defensive player.

Sometimes the person guarding you is so close that you are unable to move much. The **jab step** can help you get some space from the defender (who is "in your face") and may help you make a move on the defender, such as a crossover step and dribble.

How to Do a Jab Step

42: The Jab Step for a Lefty

- Start from the **triple-threat position**.

- For right-handed players, take a quick step forward with your right foot (as if you are going to drive to the basket).

- Left-handed players should take a step forward with their left foot.

- For righties, bring your right foot back to the triple-threat position. If this is done correctly, the defensive player may move back a little and be off balance.

The **jab step** should give you some breathing room or space between you and the defender.

Jab Step and Crossover Dribble

🏀 Once you have mastered the **jab step**, you can work on your **crossover dribble,** another powerful offensive move. The **jab step** gets the defender to move in one direction while you **cross over** and move in another direction.

 # 43: Crossover Step and Dribble

🏀 Do a **jab step** (big step) toward the right. The defensive player should take your fake and move in the direction of your fake.

🏀 Once you get back into the triple-threat position, quickly cross (move) your right foot (the one you used for the **jab step**) over to the left. As you **cross over**, dribble the ball with your left hand. A lefty should make the **jab step** with their left foot, return to the triple-threat position, and quickly cross their left foot (the one you used for the **jab step**) over to the right. As you **cross over**, dribble the ball with your right hand.

What's this "pivot foot" stuff?

You may know that you can't **walk** or **travel** (take steps) with the ball in your hands in the game of basketball.

Let's say that you are holding the ball. You are allowed to step with one of your feet in any direction—like a *jab step*.

Your other foot, called your *pivot foot*, can move or pivot, but you can't take a step with your *pivot foot*.

Don't worry; after a while you will figure out this "pivot foot" stuff.

The Ball (Shot) Fake

One of the most powerful offensive moves is the **ball fake**. This move is also known as a **shot fake** or a **pump fake**. This fake is done to get the defensive player to move backward or jump off the ground.

This move can help you get a good shot at the basket, or if the defensive player jumps off the ground, you can drive in for a layup or pull up for a jump shot.

How to Do a Ball Fake

- Start from the **triple-threat position** with the basketball.

- Make a motion to shoot. Take a step forward and raise the ball above your shoulder (remember **BPFF**—but **don't** shoot). You are faking a shot to see how the player guarding you reacts.

- Take what the defensive player gives you. If he steps back, take a shot. If he jumps up, drive to the basket.

\# 44: Fake a Drive

\# 45: Fake a Shot

Pivot Moves

Now that you have mastered the basics of footwork, let's move on to a bit more difficult footwork movements and positioning. We will cover the basic moves of **pivot and turn**, **pivot and seal**, and the **defensive slide**.

You can use a basic **pivot move** to get yourself in a position to pass, shoot, dribble, or protect the ball better with your body. Even if you don't have the ball, you can also use a **pivot move** to fake out a defender so that you can get into a better offensive position.

46: Pick a Pivot Foot, Let's Say the Right Foot

Pivoting and turning means choosing one foot to stand on while turning in different directions. Remember, once you have the ball, you are allowed to take a step with only one foot (like the **crossover** move). Your other foot is your **pivot foot**—you can turn your **pivot foot** in any direction, but you cannot pick it up off the floor.

For example, before you start dribbling or after you stop dribbling, you can move your body by pivoting and turning. One foot can come off the floor; the other foot cannot.

47: Right Pivot Foot Turns, Left Foot Turns Body

How to Pivot and Turn

- 🏀 Put all of your weight on one foot and keep your knees bent. Use the other foot to step in the direction you want to move in.

- 🏀 Always **pivot** on the balls of your feet (toward your toes), never on your heels. This will help you keep your balance.

54

- Protect the ball by keeping it close to your body with your elbows out.

- Keep your head up. Don't lean with your head forward or you may lose your balance.

Pivot and "Seal" Move

Down low (near the basket), you can use a **pivot move** to **seal** (block out) the defensive player from guarding you as you drive to the basket.

Let's say you post up near the basket, which means that you have your back to the basket and the defensive player is behind you. Give your teammate a target (hands out) to pass you the ball, making sure to keep your body between the ball and the person guarding you.

With your back to the basket, make a quick pivot fake with the right side of your body (away from the basket), pick up your left foot, and turn around toward the basket. This step toward the basket is also called a **drop step**. **Seal** (block) the defensive player as you make a move to the basket. Make the layup off the backboard with either no dribble or one low dribble.

48: Pivot Fake Right

49: Seal the Defense

Defensive Slide Step

Another important part of footwork is the defensive **slide step**. Basically, it is how you move your feet while guarding an opponent.

First, you want your feet to be spread-out wide. Your body should be between your opponent and the basket, low with your knees flexed and your eyes watching your opponent's tummy.

50: Slide Step

The **slide** part comes when the player you are guarding moves to the right or left. If he moves right (which is to your left side), you **slide** (move) your left foot first (about twelve inches) and then your right foot, always keeping your left foot about one foot from your right foot while sliding.

Make sure to keep your body between your opponent and the basket. It's like shuffling your feet to follow the player you are guarding. Do not cross your feet (right foot before left foot) while sliding.

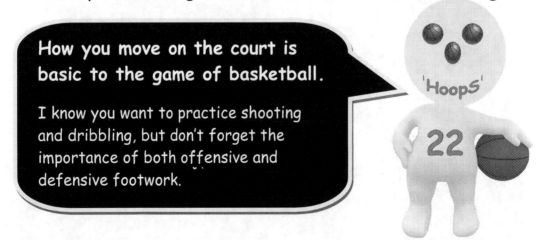

How you move on the court is basic to the game of basketball.

I know you want to practice shooting and dribbling, but don't forget the importance of both offensive and defensive footwork.

'Hoops'

22

CHAPTER 5 REBOUNDING
Sweep the boards

Rebounds happen when a team takes a shot and misses. Either team that gets possession of (has) the ball after the missed shot gets a **rebound**.

There are two types of **rebounds**: **defensive rebounds** (when the team playing defense gets the ball from a missed shot) and **offensive rebounds** (when the team that shoots the ball gets it again).

51: Go Up Strong!

Rebounding is important, because if you don't have the ball, you can't score. **Rebounding** contributes to scoring and defends against scoring. The more times your team has the ball, the more times you can shoot the ball. The fewer times the opposing team has the ball, the fewer times they can shoot the ball.

You do not have to be tall or be able to jump high to be a good rebounder. What you do need to be a good rebounder is determination, desire, good positioning, and timing.

Important *Most shots taken in a game do not go in. The team that gets more rebounds during a game has a better chance of winning that game!*

I'm a pretty short person, but I can rebound. I just follow the bouncing ball!

One trick I learned from Coach K is guessing where the ball is going to go on a missed shot so I can be in the right place at the right time.

I start out by believing that every shot will miss. I watch the shot and quickly figure out if it is going to be short or long as it goes to the basket and decide where the ball is likely to wind up. Then I move, trying to get the *inside* position on the person guarding me.

Some players take **rebounding** for granted; other players go after rebounds as if the game depended on it. If you take **rebounding** for granted, you will become a poor-to-average rebounder.

If you go after the ball with desire—"I want the ball, I need that ball"—you'll become a great rebounder. When your opponents see how much you want the ball, they'll respect you and realize that they're playing against a **ballplayer**.

Don't be afraid to yell or grunt when you **rebound**. Let everybody know you mean business and are determined to get that ball!

Many games are lost because players allow the offense to get second shots at the basket. Don't let that happen to you. If you **box out** (block out) properly, you can neutralize taller players.

58

How to Get a Defensive Rebound

● When the ball is shot, find your man or the closest person to you if you are playing a zone defense (which we will talk about later).

● Keep your back to the player and take a wide stance in front of him.

● Don't worry about the ball. At this point it is important for you to feel for your opponent with your hands or body. This way you can box (block) him out.

52: Boxing Out

● You can't push your opponent backwards: that's a foul. To keep your opponent away from the ball, you can slide to the left or right if he tries to get around you.

● Finally, when you have blocked out your man, you can go for the ball. Jump high and grab the ball with two hands and protect it with your elbows out wide.

53: Two-Handed Rebound

How to Get an Offensive Rebound

- Try to imagine where the ball is going to bounce after a missed shot:

  Shots from the right side usually miss to the left.
  Shots from the left side usually miss to the right.

- Try not to let the defensive player touch you. Go around the defensive player as you go toward the hoop. Fake him out by taking a step in one direction and going in the other direction.

- If you can't get in front of the defensive player, try to get yourself next to him.

- If you can't jump and grab the ball, try to tip it in.

- Tip it to the backboard and not the rim.

- If you do get an **offensive rebound** near the backboard, try to go right up for a layup without dribbling the ball.

How to Practice Rebounding

You can certainly practice **rebounding** by yourself; however, having a partner practice with you is even better.

Rebounding Drill 1: Stand about two feet from the basket. Throw the ball off the backboard (or wall) and jump up with your body **wide** and catch the ball with two hands. Come down with the ball with your elbows out. Do this from both sides of the basket.

Rebounding Drill 2: Do the drill from part 1 above, but after you come down with the ball, pivot (turn) and make believe you are throwing a pass (called an outlet pass) to your teammate.

Rebounding Drill 3: Do the drill from part 1 above, but after you come down with the ball, take a layup shot (and **make** it).

Remember, try not to bounce (dribble) the ball before you take the shot. Also, make sure you practice this from both the right side and the left side of the basket. Try to take a right-handed layup from the right side and a left-handed layup from the left side of the basket.

Here is a drill your mom will love—you won't wreck the house...

Blow up a balloon about the size of a basketball. It could be any color you like!

Hit the balloon high up on the wall. Jump up and catch it in the correct rebounding position.

Next, with a partner, pick an area on the floor (about ten feet by ten feet), tap the balloon in the air, and keep tapping it without your partner touching it. Both of you must stay within the play area. Protect the ball by using your body to "box out" your partner from touching the balloon (ball).

This is really hard to do, but you will be a better rebounder!

CHAPTER 6 DEFENSE
Shut them down!

There are two types of basic defense: **one-on-one defense** (man-to-man) and **team defense**. **One-on-one** defense is guarding the player you are assigned (told to guard). **Team** defense, both man-to-man and zone, is all five players on your team working together and helping each other to defend against the other team. Let's go over **one-on-one** defense now, and we will cover team defense in the **"overtime"** section of the book.

54: One-on-One Defense

Defense is hard to learn by yourself. Have your partner work with you so you can learn together.

Defense wins games! If you stop your man from scoring and your teammates do their job with each of their men, you have a better chance of winning the game. It is that simple.

How to Play One-on-One Defense

You don't have to be a great athlete to play good defense.

Defense not only involves physical ability (how fast you run or how high you jump), but mental ability as well (knowing what to do and when to do it) both as an individual player and as a team member. You can defend against a player who is bigger, stronger, or faster than you are by using your brains, your **smarts**.

In a nutshell, get *tough* like me!

To play defense you must:

- Be *aggressive* and not lazy; have the desire and determination to stop your man

- Be able to *anticipate* what your opponent is going to do and have the courage to stop him

- Use your *smarts* to play better defense. *Think!*

Practice the right defensive *stance* and *footwork* to play good, solid defense.

Hoops mentions some very important things about defense. Being aggressive and determined to play good defense comes from the heart. You have to want to stop the player you are guarding.

Being able to **anticipate** (thinking ahead, in the future) comes from really understanding the game.

Ask yourself, for example, "Where is the pass going to go next—across the court or down low? Does the player I am guarding box out correctly or is he lazy?" Do you say, "Can I get the

55: Tough Defense

inside position (between the defensive player and the basket) to rebound?"

The more you watch and play, the better you will understand the game and be able to **anticipate** (to guess what is going to happen next).

Being a smart defensive player is very important. Just as doing your school homework helps you get better grades, studying your opponent (scouting) will help you play better defense.

Asking yourself some key questions about whom you are guarding will help you play tough defense—know your opponent.

- Does he shoot well? If yes, from where on the court does he make most of his shots?

- Is he right-handed or left-handed? Can he dribble well with both hands?

- Does he dribble too high and not protect the ball? If so, can I steal the ball?

- After passing the ball does he stand still or move? Like cutting to the basket?

- Does he box out? Can I get around him into a good rebounding position?

56: Know Whom You Are Defending

How to Play One-on-One Defense

When your opponent *does not* have the ball (called *off the ball*)

- Get in the triple-threat position, which on defense is called the **defensive stance**. Put one foot slightly in front of the other and stay on the balls of your feet (with your weight toward your toes).

- Keep your head up, back straight and backside down.

- When you move, keep your knees bent and take short **sliding** steps.

- Do not cross one foot over the other when you move.

- It is important to keep one eye on the ball and one eye on your man. **Position your body so you can see your man and the player with the ball at the same time.**

- Try to make the offensive player go in a direction he doesn't want to go (we will talk about this soon).

57: Deny the Ball Outside

58: Deny the Ball Down Low

- You can use your body to help hold off a player and deny him the ball if he tries posting-up on you (setting up under the basket).

- Sometimes it's better to stay between the man and the hoop but in some situations you want to guard the passing lanes to deflect a pass or to force a lob if he is trying to post you up.

59: Defense...Head Up ...Slide Feet

When your opponent *does* have the ball (called *on the ball*)

- Get into the triple-threat position about an arm's length from the offensive player.

- **Watch the offensive player's waist**, not the ball. If you watch his waist, he will have a harder time faking you out.

- Your hands should be up to about your waist. You can hold one hand higher than the other to force a man in a direction you want him to go

60: Don't Leave Your Feet to Block Shot

- When the offensive player stops dribbling (called **picking up the dribble**), get closer to him and make it difficult for him to pass the ball or shoot. Don't touch him; that's a **foul**.

- Keep your hands moving so you can deflect a pass or stuff (block) a shot.

67

In all my years of playing bball and helping Coach K, I have learned that there is one defensive move that is critical (very, very important): how to overplay your opponent and "shut him down."

Overplaying the person you are guarding is based on a simple general fact:

Righties go right and lefties go left.

What that means is that most players cannot dribble well with both hands. Righties who can't dribble well with their left hand will dribble more with their right hand, which, if you are guarding them, is your left side.

It's hard to explain. I'll let Coach K do it!

Overplaying on Defense

Hoops is right. You must learn this defensive move. It may be difficult to understand at first, but once you understand it, you won't forget it (like riding a bike).

Go to a large mirror in your house. Put your hands up in a defensive position. Make believe that the person you see in the mirror (which is a reflection of you) is the person you are guarding.

Wiggle your **left** hand and look what happens. The person you are guarding (in the mirror) is wiggling his **right** hand. Now, hold a basketball in your left hand and look in the mirror.
The person you are guarding (in the mirror) is holding the ball in his **right** hand, which is facing **your left side**.

So, if the person you are guarding starts to dribble with his right hand, he is moving to your **left** side ... his **right is your left**.

Take your time to understand this. Once you do understand this we can talk about *overplaying* your man defensively, a very powerful tool you can use to play better and smarter defense.

61: Your Left Side...is Her Right Side

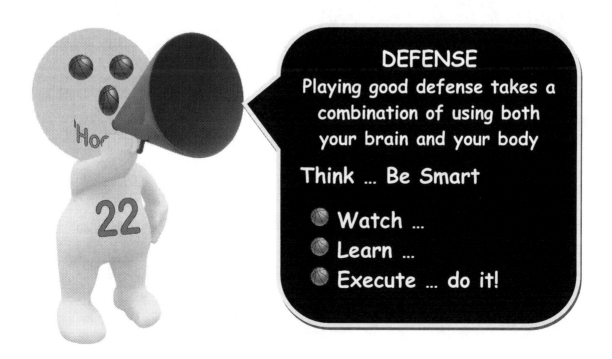

DEFENSE
Playing good defense takes a combination of using both your brain and your body

Think ... Be Smart

- Watch ...
- Learn ...
- Execute ... do it!

Overplaying your man defensively

What we know so far:

- Righties go right, and lefties go left

- Most players cannot dribble well with their weak hand (if you are a righty that would be your left hand)

- Some players who might be able to dribble with their weak hand can only do so for one or two dribbles

- If you are guarding a righty, he is likely to move and dribble to your left side

Knowing this, let's now play smart defense. Instead of guarding your opponent directly in front of you, called **straight-up defense**, play your man a half-step over to your **left**. You are now **overplaying** your opponent and making it much more difficult for him to drive to the basket against you. As your opponent moves right, you **keep overplaying** him one step to your left.

Of course, if the player you are guarding is a **lefty**, **overplay** him to your **right**. Get it? You will, and once you do it right, you will be a much better defensive player.

Straight-Up Defense

Notice the arrows in the picture. The defensive man's feet are lined up with the offensive man's feet.

This is good defense if the man you are guarding can dribble well with both hands.

Right to ➡ Left foot

Left to ➡ Right foot

Straight-Up Defense

Overplay to Your Left

Overplay Defense

If the offensive player cannot dribble well with his weak hand, in this case his left hand, the defensive player shifts his feet to prevent the offensive player from driving right. He does this by lining up his **right** foot with the the offensive player's **right** foot.

As the offensive player moves right, the defensive player slides his feet to always **overplay**.

Right to ➡ Right foot

71

CHAPTER 7 OVERTIME
Go to the next level

This chapter, **Overtime**, will cover even slightly more advanced basketball basics related to team aspects of the game. As you know, basketball is a team game where the skills of individual players are combined into a cohesive unit which means playing together as a team.

All members of the team must work together for one common goal. On **offense** it means doing everything together to help score baskets. On **defense** it means doing everything together to prevent the opposing team from scoring.

Team play is the key. A team that plays together, helping, supporting, and believing in each other, can beat a team that has great individual players, but does not play well as a team.

The two main areas we will review are **moving without the ball** on offense and the two basic team defenses: **man-to-man** and **zone.**

TEAM OFFENSE: Moving without the Ball

Having a **game** (ability to play) without the ball is a must for any player who wants to advance in basketball. Consider that the average player spends about 95 percent of his time during a game without the ball. Players must develop skills that will enable them to receive the ball in a most favorable (good) scoring position.

The key elements of moving without the ball are **change of pace** and **change of direction**. These are crucial movements in developing an effective game without the ball.

● **Change of Pace:** Run slow, run fast, run slow, run fast...stop and go, stop and go. Any offensive player is quicker than his defensive opponent without the ball for the first two steps after a change of pace. The more dramatic the change, the more open a player is likely to be to receive a pass

● **Change of Direction:** A basic rule for getting open without the ball is to avoid going in a straight line to the ball. Each player must learn to play with his knees bent and his body in a good balance to change direction. The most common cuts are the **V** cut (where you run a few steps, stop, change direction and run some more, like the letter **V**) and the **give and go** cut (you pass the ball to a teammate and quickly run to the basket).

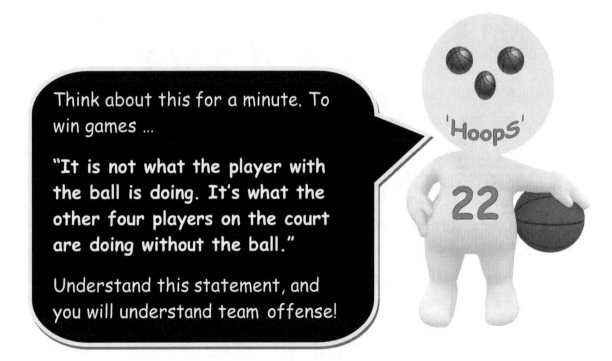

Think about this for a minute. To win games ...

"It is not what the player with the ball is doing. It's what the other four players on the court are doing without the ball."

Understand this statement, and you will understand team offense!

Now it is time to introduce you to a **coach's clipboard.**

A **coach's clipboard** (which has a picture of a basketball court on it) is used by coaches to diagram (show) where players should move and what to do on the court. Most coaches use the board to diagram plays. It is important to understand what is being shown on the board.

Let's map out a **give and go** and a **V** cut on the clipboard and show the play with some pictures. Before we do that, we need a **key** (a code) to understanding what is going on.

Let's use the **clipboard key** to understand two basic moves without the ball—the **give and go** and the **V cut** and **pick**.

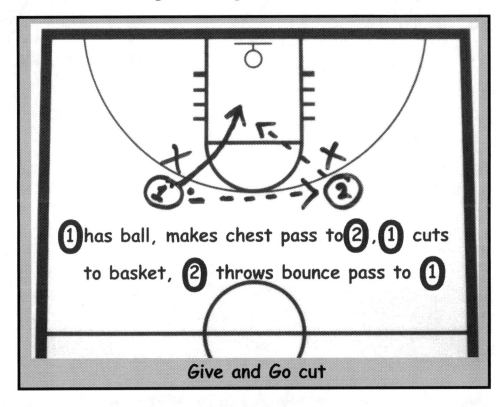

①has ball, makes chest pass to ②, ① cuts to basket, ② throws bounce pass to ①

Give and Go cut

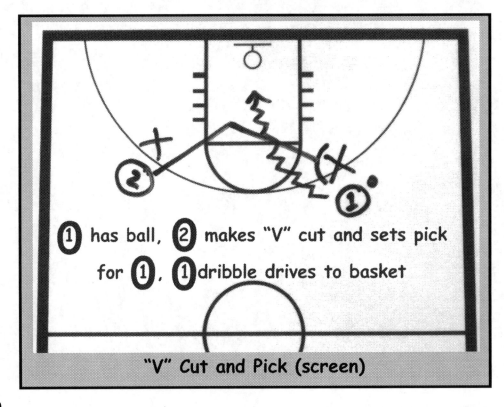

① has ball, ② makes "V" cut and sets pick for ①, ① dribble drives to basket

"V" Cut and Pick (screen)

Setting a Pick or a Screen

Moving without the ball often involves the setting of a **pick** (another word meaning a **block** or **screen**) so that your teammate can get open for a shot or pass. Most picks are made (set) against a man-to-man defense.

Let's talk about a **simple pick**. Say your teammate has the ball and is being guarded closely by the defender. To set a block, you would make a **V** cut and come up from the side and block-out the defender.

Your teammate would then be able to use your **pick**, since you blocked out the player guarding him, and he is free to dribble and drive to the basket.

62: Pick for Cut without Ball

63: Pick for Cut with Ball

How to Set and Use Screens and Picks

Key points for *setting* a screen

- Screens can be used (set) for teammates who either have the ball or do not have the ball.

- Once you set a pick, you have to stay in that position for three seconds or until the pick is used by your teammate.

- Place your arms close to your body with your knees slightly bent.

- Set the pick about one step away from the defender.

- You know you set the screen correctly when the defender knocks into you as he tries to guard his player.

- Don't push the defender—that's a foul. Don't move once you have set the pick.

Key points for *using* a screen

\# 64: Pick for Drive

- Before the screen is set for you, get as close as possible to your defender. The closer you are to the person guarding you, the better the chance you have of getting free.

- Wait for the pick to come to you (be set) before you move. A screen is not much help if you move before it is set.

- Once the pick is set, make a sharp cut (not wide) past your teammate's shoulder.

Two of the most basic offensive plays are the **pick and roll** and the **C** play.

The Pick and Roll

The **pick and roll**, when done correctly, is one of the most powerful offensive skills a team can learn. It is very hard to defend against and can be used just about anywhere on the court.

65: Use Pick and Drive

You and your teammates must all use good footwork, communicate with each other, set the correct picks and use the screen the right way: all of the skills we have already talked about. There is one additional feature (skill) to this play—the **roll**. After you set the pick you **roll** or move to the basket for a possible pass or rebound.

66: Screener "Rolls" to Basket

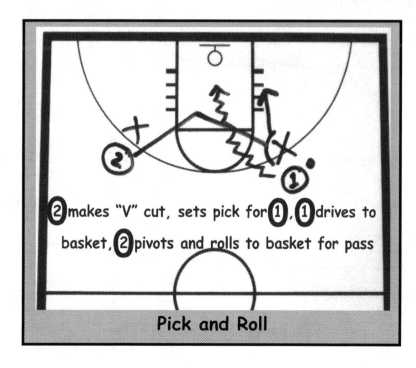
②makes "V" cut, sets pick for ①, ①drives to basket, ②pivots and rolls to basket for pass

Pick and Roll

79

The "C" Play

Another offensive play is the "C" play or **pass and pick away** (from the ball). It is not really a play, but an **offensive set**, a pattern, that a team can use often and in many different ways against a man-to-man defense.

The play integrates (uses) all of the basic skills we have learned so far and puts them together in an organized way.

67: Pass and Set Pick Away

The pattern of **pass and pick away** sounds simple, but a team must practice this to get all the parts working together correctly.

The pattern is that the player with the ball passes to another teammate and then sets a pick away from the ball.

68: Pick Is Set Away from Ball

If the pass is made to a teammate on the right side of the court, the passer sets a screen on the left side of the court.

The offensive player who had the pick set for him **cuts** (moves) to the basket for a pass to either drive in for a layup or shoot a short pull-up (off the dribble) jump shot.

69: Cut to Basket Using Pick

"C" Play on Coach's Clipboard

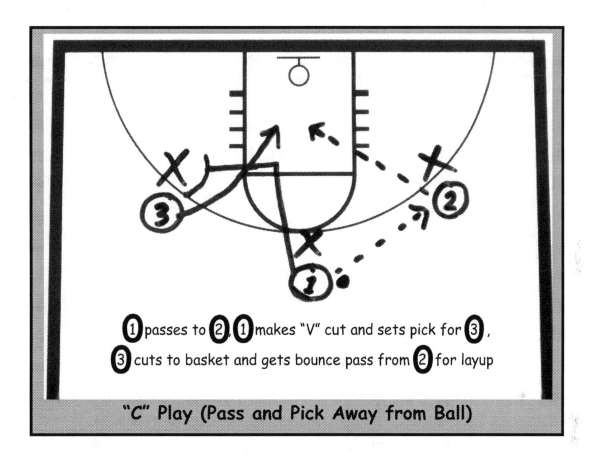

1 passes to 2, 1 makes "V" cut and sets pick for 3,
3 cuts to basket and gets bounce pass from 2 for layup

"C" Play (Pass and Pick Away from Ball)

'HoopS

So, you think you know all this *moving without the ball* stuff like cuts, picks, and rolls. Let's see...

What should the player who set the pick do after he sets the pick?

What should the player who passed the ball do after he passes the ball?

Can you map-out on a separate piece of paper a "C" play?

TEAM DEFENSE

If you remember, we talked about one-on-one defense in Chapter 6. Now we are going to turn our attention to **team defense**.

There are two basic team defenses: **man-to-man** and **zone**. There are many variations (different types) of these defenses. Sometimes they are combined, and a team plays both at the same time. Regardless of which defense is used, your individual skills on defense are very important, but now you are combining those skills with those of your teammates.

Remember the expression, **"Defense wins games."** How true this is! The team that plays together and does not let the opposing team score more points than they do will win the game!

Our goal here is to keep it simple so that you understand the basics of each defense and can apply these concepts (the idea of how things should work) to any variation (a change from the original).

Just to refresh your memory, a **man-to-man** defense is where each defensive player has an opposing player to guard, and a **zone** defense has each player defending an area on the court, not a specific offensive player.

70: Keep your Eyes on the Man You Are Guarding (Who Does Not Have the Ball), and the Man with the Ball

Regardless of which defense you play, you must always be in position to see the man or area you are guarding and the ball.

Each type of defense has its own advantages and disadvantages. The type of defense you play depends upon the strengths and weaknesses of your team and the opponents' team. For example, if the team you are playing is much faster than your team, a **zone** might be better to use than a **man-to-man** defense.

Man-to-Man Defense

Man-to-man defense is the most often used type of defense. The concept is simple. Each of the five defensive players on the court is told to guard a specific offensive player.

Each of the defensive players must try to stop his assigned offensive player from scoring a basket, making a good pass, or getting an offensive rebound. Together, as a team, if all the

#71: Man-to-Man Defense

players do this, the team is playing good **man-to-man defense**.

The Basics of Man-to-Man Defense

- Your job is clear—guard a specific offensive player
- Make it difficult for that player to score, dribble, pass, cut, or rebound
- Help your teammates when you can, but remember that you are responsible for the person you are guarding

The Zone Defense

A **zone defense** is where defensive players on the team are guarding an **area** (a spot) on the court, not an individual offensive player. If an offensive player comes into the area you are guarding, you are then responsible for guarding that player.

Generally, the **zone defense** shifts (moves) in the direction of where the ball is. If the ball is on the right side of the court (looking at the basket), the defense shifts to their left (remember that from individual defensive movement?).

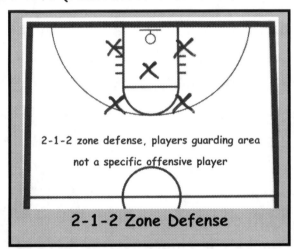

2-1-2 zone defense, players guarding area not a specific offensive player

2-1-2 Zone Defense

To understand this better, let's talk about the most basic **zone defense**, the 2-1-2 zone. You will note from the **coach's clipboard** that the defensive players (the **X's**) are guarding areas on the court and not specific players. Most zone defenses are used to **clog-up** the middle and take away the drive to the basket. This type of defense attempts to force the offense to take outside shots from far away in the hope they don't make too many.

 # 72: The 2-1-2 Zone

In addition to forcing the offensive team to shoot perimeter shots (shots far from the basket), a team may also use a **zone defense** to protect players in foul trouble. Since you are not playing a specific offensive player, you are less likely to commit a foul.

84

Teams may also use a zone to neutralize (take away an advantage) an opposing team that is much faster or bigger than your team.

The Basics of a Zone Defense

● You must get back on defense quickly and set up your zone.

● You must know where the ball is at all times, and shift into your defensive position properly.

 # 73: Zone Shifts to Ball

● All players on the defensive team have to communicate with each other. For example, "Watch the **cutter** (player) going to the basket."

● When a shot is taken, all defensive players must box out any opposing player in their area.

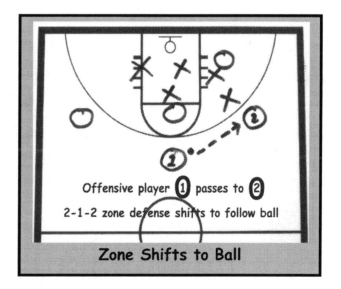

Offensive player ① passes to ②
2-1-2 zone defense shifts to follow ball

Zone Shifts to Ball

● Keep the zone "tight" (clogging-up the middle); don't let anyone get an easy layup.

CHAPTER 8 TIME OUT

Some extra "goodies"

This chapter, **TIME OUT**, will go over some **extra goodies** that are important for you to be a good ballplayer. First, some thoughts are offered on **Nutrition**—eating. **Warming up, stretching and cooling down** are next. They are important for you to know about to play the game in a safe way. Also, a **sixty-minute plan** for practicing your hoops regularly is mapped out. Finally, the chapter ends with a fun quiz testing your knowledge of the game.

NUTRITION

As you can see, I like to eat!

I snack a lot, love candy bars, drool over ice cream sundaes, and can't wait for a double burger.

You can love munching a burger and fries with your friends. It all tastes so good! But just don't eat too much. It will slow you down when you're shooting hoops.

You want a snack? Earn it with a workout!

It is important to talk a bit about healthy eating habits. Proper nutrition and regular physical activity can help you get in shape and feel good about yourself and, of course, be a better ballplayer.

- Eat only when you are hungry
- Don't eat between meals
- Don't overeat. Eat to be satisfied not stuffed

Remember *What you eat is also very important. I'm sure you hear about this in school and at home. Just eat a balanced diet and run around a lot, and you'll be okay.*

87

STRETCHING EXERCISES: Warm up, Cool down

Almost every person playing sports today stretches and loosens-up their muscles before actually playing. Why bother to do this? Why not just get on the court and play?

The answer is simple—getting your body **ready** to play will keep you from getting hurt **when** you play. A sprained ankle, a pulled muscle, or a strained back hurts. Loosening up before playing can help stop you from getting hurt so you can keep playing and have more fun.

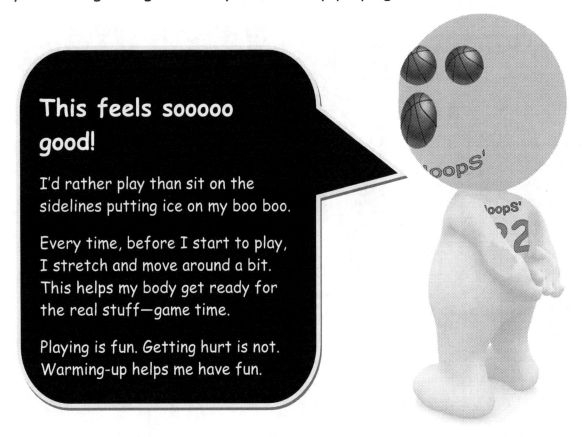

This feels sooooo good!

I'd rather play than sit on the sidelines putting ice on my boo boo.

Every time, before I start to play, I stretch and move around a bit. This helps my body get ready for the real stuff—game time.

Playing is fun. Getting hurt is not. Warming-up helps me have fun.

I'm sure you have seen on TV or in-person players, at all levels from little kids to professional athletes, loosening up before a game. It is important that you **warm up** and **stretch** correctly before you do a basketball workout and **cool down** after the workout.

Warm up: Prior to stretching, do five minutes of general movement (for example, run around a little while swinging your arms in all directions). This will get the blood moving and warm the muscles and other parts of your body before you stretch.

Stretching: It is very important that you stretch the right way. Various stretching exercises good for basketball are shown on the next pages.

I chose six stretching excercises to share with you with instructions on how to do them. Study the pictures shown while you read the instructions. Try it. Before you know it, you will be stretching like a "pro."

Stretching is the recognized Bible of stretching exercises for various activities.

My thanks to Shelter Publications Inc. for permitting me to use these exercises from the book *Stretching* by Bob and Jean Anderson (30th Anniversary Edition, 2010). For more good stretches and useful info, please check out *Stretching.*

Cool down: After you finish playing, do five minutes of general movement. This will help prevent muscle soreness and stiffness.

Selected Stretches for Basketball

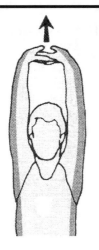

Put your fingers together (interlaced like laces) above your head and, with your palms facing upward, push your arms up and slightly back.

Hold your arms this way and count for ten seconds (1 one hundred, 2 one hundred ... ten one hundred). Take deep breaths while counting. Do it again.

This stretches the arms, shoulders, and upper back.

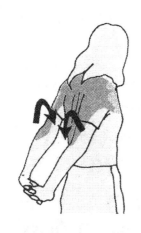

Put your hands behind your back. Fingers should be interlaced behind your back.

Turn your elbows inward while straightening your arms. Your palms should be facing downward

Hold for five to ten seconds. Breathe deeply. Repeat.

This stretches the shoulders, arms, and chest.

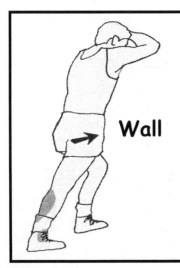

Wall

Lean on the wall with your forearms and your elbows touching the wall. Rest your head on your hands. Bend one leg and place your foot on the ground in front of you, with your other leg straight behind.

Slowly lean forward, keeping your lower back flat. Try to keep your heels on ground.

Hold for ten to fifteen seconds. Switch legs.

This stretches the legs, hips, and calves.

Selected Stretches for Basketball

Sit down on the floor. Straighten your right leg with the sole (bottom) of your left foot slightly touching the inside of your right thigh. Slowly bend forward.

Hold for five to ten seconds. Switch sides and stretch your left leg.

This stretches the hamstring which is the muscle behind your leg above the knee.

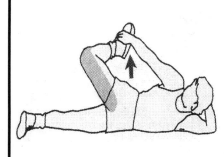

Lie down on your left side and rest your head in the palm of your left hand.

Hold the top of your right foot with your right hand. Gently pull your right heel toward your buttock.

Hold for ten seconds. Repeat with your other leg.

This stretches your ankle and thigh.

Lie on your back and pull your left leg toward your chest. Keep your head down and your other leg straight.

Hold for twenty seconds. Repeat with your other leg.

This stretches the back muscles and the hamstrings.

Bball basics PRACTICING YOUR HOOPS

This sixty-minute plan will help you practice your hoop skills. If you can do the full sixty-minute plan, great. If not, do half one day and half the next day. As an added bonus, after you are done, take twenty foul shots. And remember ... **expect** to make those shots!

ITEM	MINUTES	SKILL	DESCRIPTION of ACTION
1	5	**Passing** (see pages 25-28)	Pass the ball off a wall. Practice both the chest pass and the bounce pass. Catch the pass in a **triple-threat position**.
2	5	**Dribbling** (see pages 17-22)	Using correct form, dribble forward, backward, stop, start, change speeds.
3	5	**Layups** (see pages 46-48)	Shoot thirty layups in five minutes. Starting from the right side of the basket, dribble once and then make a layup. Rebound, go to the left side, take one dribble, and do a lefty layup.
4	5	**Inter-mediate Shots** (see pages 33-45)	Starting ten feet from the basket, take a shot and rebound before the ball touches the ground. Take ten shots. Starting fifteen feet from basket, make ten shots from different areas on the court.

ITEM	MINUTES	SKILL	DESCRIPTION of ACTION
5	5	**Footwork Defensive Slides** 3 Steps (see page 56)	Assuming the correct defensive stance, go forward three steps, stop on **balance**, take three steps backward, slide three steps to the right, and slide three steps to the left. Do this again.
6	5	**Footwork Defensive Slides** 6 Steps	Same as above, but take six steps
7	5	**Rebounding** (see pages 57-61)	Jump as high as you can with both hands up; land in **balance**. Repeat four times. Rest ten seconds, and repeat again.
8	10	**Rebounding Control**	Throw the ball off the backboard; rebound with two hands. Land in **balance**. Repeat and, after landing, **pivot to pass**.
9	5	**Offensive Rebound** (see page 60)	Standing five feet from basket, throw the ball high off the backboard, run in, catch the ball, and shoot a layup. Rest; repeat. Take both righty and lefty layups.
10	10	**Court Sprints**	Sprint the full length of court at full speed and return walking at moderate speed. Repeat; rest; repeat.

Bball basics Mini-Quiz Questions		Answers on Next Page
1	How far from the backboard is the foul line?	
2	What is the defense called when players on the defensive team are guarding an "area"?	
3	What do NBA and WNBA stand for?	
4	Approximately, what is a diameter of a boy's basketball?	
5	If you make two foul shots, how many points have you scored?	
6	What violation have you made if you pick up your pivot foot after you stop dibbling?	
7	What year was the game of basketball created and who invented it?	
8	What does "BPFF" stand for?	
9	Let's say you are guarding a player who is driving to the basket dribbling with his right hand. What direction should you slide your feet to guard him?	
10	If you dribble with both hands at once you will be called for this violation?	
11	What is another word for blocking-out your opponent for a rebound?	
12	I'm the one spot, the playmaker of the team. What am I called?	
13	What is the official height of the basket off the ground?	
14	What kind of ball was first used to play the game of basketball?	
15	When a teammate throws you a pass, you should catch it in what type of a position?	
16	What is the defense called when each of the five defensive players on the court is assigned to guard a specific offensive player?	
17	Name the lane where you can't "hang out" for too long?	
18	What is the size of the official high school basketball court?	
19	What are offensive mistakes (like traveling, three-seconds, having a pass stolen) called?	
20	What letter of the alphabet describes a "move without the ball"?	

Bball basics Answer Sheet

A. James A. Naismith invented basketball in 1891.

B. First ball used in basketball was a soccer ball.

C. Man-to-man defense

D. Zone defense

E. 9 1/2" diameter

F. Three-second Lane

G. The National Basketball Association and the
   Women's National Basketball Association

H. Court is 84 feet long, 50 feet wide

I. Two points

J. Turnovers

K. B= Balance, P= Pointy Finger, F= Flip,
   and F= Follow-Through

L. The letter "V" for "V" cut

M. A travel or walking violation

N. Fifteen feet

O. Triple-threat Position

P. A double-dribble violation

Q. Boxing out

R. Ten feet

S. You should slide your feet to your left.

T. A Point Guard

Let's have fun with this quiz...I'll give you the answers... you match them to the questions.

I'm not matching them up for you... You can figure this out !

CHAPTER 9 INSPIRATIONAL STORIES

INSPIRATIONAL STORY #1: *Hang in There*

For thirteen years, I had the joy of owning and directing a sleep-over basketball summer camp. During those years of running the camp, I met a few kids who attended the camp who had little interest in getting better in basketball. So you might ask, "What were they doing in a basketball camp?" This story may help answer the question.

One such camper by the name of Sammy was not especially athletic. He was overweight and could not jump high or run fast. In fact, he could not jump at all or jog for more than a few steps. He had never played basketball in the past, and it was a wonder that he was actually signed up for a basketball camp program.

Sometimes parents send a child to a camp that is not the right place for that kid to spend a summer. Often parents think that sending their child to a camp specializing in basketball (or any other sport) will automatically produce an athlete. This usually does not happen, and the child could be miserable and blame his parents for putting him in an embarrassing and frustrating place. The child often has a feeling of not belonging or not being able to get better compared to other children with better athletic abilities. It's just not fun to be in a serious basketball camp when you are not into the game!

Sammy was in a tough spot and had to make a decision—he could be miserable, complain and make life difficult for himself, fellow campers and staff, or suck it up and make the best of the situation. Let's see what Sammy did.

The camp had team practice in the afternoon after a morning of stretching with skill workouts and drills. Sammy had trouble keeping up with the morning workouts, and he got tired quickly. In fact, to help himself stretch, Sammy made believe he was stretching up to pluck a Snickers bar hanging off an imaginary branch of a tree.

All the kids were placed on teams with a coach and practiced team defense, offense, out-of-bounds plays, and so on. Basketball activities continued in the evenings with games between the teams that practiced during the day. During the games, the campers were urged to try out any new skills they had learned in the morning (like dribbling with your weak hand). Campers practiced and played basketball for over six hours a day.

Sammy knew he would never be a good basketball player, but he hung in there and kept going. Sammy could have given up and quit. He did not! As the summer moved along, Sammy's fellow campers began to respect Sammy for his effort, determination, and smile. Sammy knew it would all work out. And it did, especially one beautiful summer evening.

That evening, Sammy's team was playing, and I was refereeing the game. Sammy wore his basketball uniform just like his teammates. Sammy "huddled up" with his teammates to hear his coach give last minute instructions before the start of the game. Sammy cheered for his teammates and listened carefully to his coach during time outs. He even got into the game a few times since my rule for the camp was that all players play about equal time during the games. To Sammy's credit, he did try hard to keep up with the fast-paced action of the game.

In this particular game, Sammy's team was losing by two points, and time was running out. With about five seconds remaining in the game, Sammy threw up a shot from behind the three-point line. We all watched as the ball arched upward toward the basket. Just as the ball dropped through the basket, the buzzer sounded, ending the game. Sammy had hit the winning basket! His arms were raised up in celebration as his teammates danced joyfully around him. Even the opposing team joined in celebrating with Sammy on his winning shot. During the happy mob scene, Sammy's eyes met mine; I then knew why Sammy stuck it out and succeeded in a basketball camp.

For one summer Sammy was part of a team, wore a basketball uniform, and had a coach—just like a real ballplayer. He felt that he belonged after all. For one golden moment on the basketball court, Sammy achieved a great feat—he was "the man."

After camp, I never saw Sammy again. But every summer I receive an e-mail from Sammy. The e-mail is the same every year—one sentence long: "Do you remember my shot?" I reply each time with "I will never forget it!" Apparently, Sammy will never forget it either.

This story proves that anyone who puts his mind to it can take on a challenging situation and make the best of it. Sammy's efforts were not wasted, and with that game-winning experience, he came away with a good feeling about himself that he will carry with him for the rest of his life. And it was a great positive learning experience for every camper and staff member as well.

INSPIRATIONAL STORY #2: *You Never Know*

We usually don't realize it, but something we do or say today may have great importance five or ten years in the future.

If you make fun of a fellow student today, you may think it's no big deal, but that kid may never forget what you said or did to him. Ten or twenty years from now you may want a job and that very same person may be doing the hiring. You probably won't get the job because that kid, who is now an adult, has not forgotten how you embarrassed him many years ago.

On the other hand, if you say or do something good and positive to someone they probably will not forget that you were a good guy and you may benefit—years later—from being nice. You never know!

I was fortunate to play a really good game that helped my team win my high school basketball championship. I remember shaking hands with the players we beat and their coach telling me "good game." Years later it was a pleasant memory for me, but I had no idea that the game, and my performance in it, would somehow benefit my brother in a really good way many years later. You never know!

During the mid-1960s, the United States was involved in the Vietnam War, halfway around the world from America. I was still in high school then, but I do remember my family watching the TV evening news reports. Every day the news ended with the reporter telling how many American soldiers were killed that day and how many soldiers had been killed in total since the beginning of the war. Every day the number of soldiers killed or wounded got higher and higher.

I was just a kid, more interested in playing ball and having fun and not really understanding what the war was all about. As a teenager, I certainly did not relate to the difficult times families were having while their children were in the army being trained to fight and shoot guns in the jungles of Vietnam. Many families worried that their child would be killed or return wounded from the war.

My brother, Joel, who is four years older than me, was drafted and picked to serve in the US Army. It's important to tell you that we look very much alike. He was sent to a large army base with tens of thousands of others to be trained as soldiers.

My brother, who had never shot a gun in his life, was taken to a shooting range to learn and practice how to fire a rifle. As luck would have it, my brother hit the target!

The army said, "Wow, good shot! We are going to train you to be a 'marksman,' a sharp shooter—someone really good at hitting the target." His job in Vietnam would be to defend his country on the front line right in the middle of danger. He would have to hike deep in the jungle, climb a tree, and radio back to army headquarters where the "bad" guys (i.e., the enemy) were hiding. The soldier who was assigned this job had a high possibility of not returning from the jungle alive.

Although I did not understand it at the time, when faced with danger and the chances of being shot at and possibly killed, many people turn to God for guidance and comfort.

My brother Joel was no exception. With two weeks left before his army group was due to depart for Vietnam, my brother realized that it was time to prepare for this dangerous mission by visiting an army chaplain on base. A chaplain is a priest, minister, or rabbi who is part of the army and is there to help guide the soldiers spiritually as needed.

My brother decided that this would be the best way to remind the Almighty that he was going to war with a request and prayer to watch over him.

Now, as I mentioned before, my brother and I look alike. Fortunately, an interesting thing happened that shaped my brother's future. Joel walked into the chaplain's office, and before he sat down to talk, the chaplain said, "You look very familiar." They started talking and discovered that the chaplain was the basketball coach of the team that my school defeated in that championship game a few years before. Remember, in that game, I played very well, scoring fourteen points while defensively shutting down the star player of his team. It was not surprising for the opposing coach (now a chaplain) to remember me years later.

The basketball connection helped my brother and the chaplain to have a nice friendly talk, and they hit it off. As fate would have it, the chaplain was looking to fill a key helper position and offered my brother the job on the spot. Without hesitation, my brother took the job. In the end, although he never was shipped out to Vietnam and never shot a gun again in his life, he admirably served his country as a chaplain's assistant.

It's interesting how things have a way of working out. I am convinced that my solid basketball skills developed after years of practice played a major role in this story. I was destined to play well in that championship game and with good sportsmanship—well enough that the opposing coach, who became chaplain later on, remembered me.

So remember, what you do and say one year can influence things in a good or bad way years later. You can't go wrong by trying to be respectful and nice to others. As the saying goes, "You never know!"

INSPIRATIONAL STORY #3: *Stick to Your Game Plan*

After volunteering my time coaching for many years at community centers and local elementary schools, I was offered my first paid high school varsity basketball head-coaching job. The pay was not so much, but I was getting paid for doing something that I loved to do.

The boy's varsity team's regular season record the year before I took over as coach was a disappointing six wins and ten defeats. I did have a chance to see the team play in their final game of the season before I took over the coaching job. Although the team lost their last game, I saw good individual talent but noticed almost no sense of teamwork. The team seemed to have no clue about what to do on the court and just played as if they were five guys doing their own thing. I could not wait to put my coaching ideas into play the following year.

Tryouts for my first season in high school coaching went well, and I chose sixteen players for the team. We worked hard, and with a little luck, the team slowly began to play basketball the right way—with a sense of purpose and teamwork. As the season moved on, we kept getting better and better with every game and practice. We were not a pushover team anymore—in fact, we began to believe in ourselves and actually made the play-offs along with eight other teams.

Our record was eleven wins and five losses—quite an improvement from the year before. This group of sixteen talented young men was turning into a real team

The usual way play-offs work is that the teams that make the play-offs play against each other—if you lose you're out; if you win you continue to play.

With eight teams making the play-offs, the first round of games is called the quarter-finals. The four winning teams then play in the next round, called the semi-finals. Finally, the two winning teams then play for the championship.

Any coach will tell you that it is possible for any team in the play-offs to win. It does not matter who is considered to be the better team. Upsets happen—meaning the team that is not as good as the other team, can, on any given night, beat the team expected to win. That is the beauty of sports. If the favored team always won, we would not be playing the game.

Our first quarter-final play-off game was a home game. It went down to the wire, but we won in triple overtime. Most of the starting players from both teams fouled out, but my substitute players were holding their own. We were down by two points with seven seconds to go. I called my last time out. I turned toward a kid named Ari, the last guy on my bench. He was a great shooter in practice but not in games. He simply got very nervous and was afraid to fail when he got into a game and, because of that, did not play well.

During the time out, I showed the team a simple pick play to free Ari up for a three-point shot. I looked at Ari and said, "Just make believe this is practice— shoot and make it." And he did! We won at the buzzer. Although Ari did not play much in games, his contribution in those seven seconds made his season as well as the team's.

On to the semi-finals—the next play-off round! We played our rivals from across the Hudson River. Fifteen hundred people packed the gym, which was built to hold only one thousand.

The place was rocking, and the noise from the fans of both schools was deafening. The buzzer ending the game sounded, and my team won by seven—once again, with a great team effort. Unbelievable—we were going to the championship!

The championship game was played before a New York Knicks game in Madison Square Garden (also known as MSG). We were up against a powerhouse team led by three great all-star players. This was a team that had beaten us badly twice during the regular season. This was not going to be easy.

Playing in Madison Square Garden presents its own challenges and problems to overcome. The arena is gigantic (it can hold twenty thousand people—very different from a high school gym). Just the feeling of this place, the most famous court in the world, the mecca of basketball, can be very scary and frightening, let alone actually playing a game there. The basketball court that the pros play on is ten feet longer than a high school court—that's a lot!

Before the big game, I did my homework. I spoke to older players who had played their high school basketball championship game at MSG, and each one gave me the same information (which is called a scouting report)—it is hard to shoot from the outside because the place is so big and you tire very quickly from all the excitement, hoopla, and larger court size.

We expected to have two thousand fans from both schools attending the game in a building that can hold ten times that amount. I was also told that when you shoot in such a large arena, your shot would be off because it is hard to judge how far away the basket is since the place is so enormous.

I thought about how I could use these two very important pieces of information to help my team win. We had two practices before the game and we talked about the scouting report. Since we were told it is hard to shoot outside shots, we decided to play a "packed-in" 2-1-2 zone.

This kind of defense, which has players guarding areas on the court and not man-to-man, should help stop shooting close to the basket. But, if we "pack it in" and have players playing defense even closer to the basket, the opposing team will have open outside shots. We decided to let the other team shoot! They won't make too many.

The second important piece of information—of getting tired very quickly at the beginning of the game—took some more thinking. My thoughts were to remove the starters from the game after three minutes of play and give them a rest for two minutes before putting them back into the game. My team was not comfortable with this idea and raised their eyebrows at this suggestion. But, we agreed to follow this game plan.

Kids, you should know that all plans do not work out the way you think they will. In life, there is a big difference between a theory—what you expect to happen—and reality—what really happens!

Everything leading up to the game was very exciting. My school had a "pep rally" before the game, which got everyone, including students, teachers, parents, family, and, of course, my players all fired up. The school got a big fancy "coach" bus to take the team from our school in New Jersey to New York City and Madison Square Garden—no regular school bus for us on this big day! The school even hired a photographer and video man to take pictures of this big moment. Wow!

Our locker room was right next to the New York Knicks locker room. Some of the Knick players were there and wished our team luck. Some even said that they would come out and watch our game. You could see, just warming up before the game, that this was something very special.

Okay, let's get to the game and what actually happened—reality. Within the first three minutes of the game we were down 13-2. The scouting report about shooting was only half right. My team and not the other team had a problem shooting from the outside. Nothing went in for us, but it seemed that every shot went in for the other guys!

The second idea, our theory about getting very tired at the beginning of the game, was right on the mark—both teams were exhausted. After three minutes into the game I had a big coaching decision to make.

Do we follow our game plan, which the whole team understood and bought into? Or, since the score was a lopsided 13-2 at the time, do I keep my very tired but more skilled starting five players in the game? I was very nervous, but I had to make a split-second choice.

I gulped, made the tough decision, and chose to follow the game plan. Without calling for a time out, because I did not want the opposing team to get any rest, I made the planned five substitutions. I reminded the subs that we needed two minutes of solid basketball before returning the starters to the game.

On their first play, our subs did a perfect "C" play (which is described on page 80 of this book) and scored on an easy layup. For the next two minutes, my fresh subs held the exhausted opposing team to no points while scoring six points for our side.

With three minutes left in the first quarter, I put my starters back in, slapped the back of every sub coming out of the game, and watched as my refreshed team ran fast break after fast break against an exhausted opponent. My team went on to win 65–59.

Because of hard work and a belief in each other, the team that seemed not too good, an underdog, at the start of the season became champions in the end. Not all game plans can be followed from theory to reality, but if you do your homework and believe in your plan—stick to it! It's a lesson you'll learn to live by for the rest of your life.

A FINAL WORD | Huddle-up

Team Meeting: Let's *huddle-up*

After each game or practice, most coaches meet with their teams to review what went right and what went wrong. Based on how things went, some coaches may map out what the team needs to do at the next practice to improve its skill level. Coaches and players must study why a mistake was made and figure out how to correct it. Many coaches will include what I call "housekeeping" items such as, when the next practice is or where the next game is taking place.

We should end this book with a team meeting, mapping-out your next steps to becoming a better basketball player. First, you have to ask yourself, "Am I willing to put the time and effort into improving my game?" In basketball, as in most things in life, it takes hard work, stamina, and determination to get better. And, as in life, not everything is going to go just right. You will make mistakes—everybody does. It's important to establish from the get-go that we learn from our mistakes and that's a good thing.

109

Basketball is a great game because it reflects real-life situations. Just as you can correct a mistake in playing basketball, you can do the same in life.

A player is part of a team effort that tries to, within a common set of rules, succeed in reaching a goal. The values of cooperation, the balancing of individual and team objectives, the need to trust and sacrifice, the realization of facing up to disappointments, and the understanding that actions have consequences (the results of your actions) all contribute to the experience of life!

I hope you enjoyed Bball basics !

Well, all that was easy!
Now have *fun!*

Bball basics Glossary of Basketball Terms

- **Assist:** Passing the ball to a teammate to help score a basket

- **Backboard:** A rectangular board to which the basket (rim) is attached

- **Bank Shot:** Scoring a basket with the help of the backboard

- **Basket:** The circular rim that is attached to the backboard and is ten feet high off the court. Each basket scored can be worth one point (foul shot), two points (regular shot), or three points (three-point shot).

- **Basketball:** A sport in which a round ball is used to score points by placing it in the basket. Each team consists of five players, and the game is played following specific rules and guidelines.

- **Bball:** Another term for basketball

- **Bounce Pass:** A type of pass in which the basketball bounces once on the floor before reaching a teammate's hands

- **Boxing Out:** Blocking out an opponent in order to get the rebound after a shot

- **Chest Pass:** A type of pass in which the basketball is thrown in a straight line (no bounce) from one teammate's chest area to another

- **Coach:** The leader of the team who teaches skills and makes important decisions about practice and games

- **Court:** The area basketball is played on—usually a hardwood floor or an asphalt-type playground

- **Crossover Dribble:** Switching off one's dribble from the right to left hand or from the left to right hand

- **Defense:** Preventing an opponent from scoring

- **Defensive Rebound:** A rebound by a defensive player after the opposing team shoots

- **Double Dribble:** A violation when a player stops his dribble and then dribbles again or a player uses two hands at once to dribble

- **Double Team:** When two defensive players guard one person on the opposing team

- **Dribbling/Dribble:** Bouncing the basketball on the court without stopping unless shooting or passing

- **Drill:** The practice of a specific skill (e.g. dribbling, shooting, passing)

- **Drive:** When a player dribbles toward the basket for a layup or inside shot

- **Dunk/Dunk Shot:** Jumping high above the rim to push the basketball into the basket

- **Fast Break:** Quickly moving the ball down the court (by passing or dribbling) to score before the other team can set up their defense

- **Foul:** Personal and physical contact with opposing team that is judged to be against the rules and results in a foul shot or other team's possession

- **Foul Line** (also called the *free-throw line*): The line that is fifteen feet from the backboard from which foul shots are taken

Foul Shot (also called *free throw*): After a player is fouled, the shot he or she may take from the foul line; worth one point each

Hoop/Hoops: Another name for basket or basketball

In bounds: When the basketball is in play and the clock starts

Jump Ball: When two players from opposing teams jump to tap the basketball to their teammate after the referee throws it up in the air at mid-court. This happens both at the start of a game and to begin an overtime period.

Jump Shot: A shot taken when a player is in the air

Layup: A shot taken when a player, near the basket, shoots the basketball over the rim or against the backboard to score

Man-to-Man Defense: A type of defense where each player guards a "man" (a person) on the opposing team rather than an area (zone defense)

NBA/WNBA: The National Basketball Association and the Women's National Basketball Association (professional basketball)

NCAA: The National Collegiate Athletic Association

Net: Material attached to the rim of the basket that the basketball goes through

Offense: The team that has possession of the basketball and tries to score against the opposing team

Offensive Rebound: Getting a rebound after a teammate shoots the basketball

Official: Another word for referee

Overtime (OT): Extra time added to the end of a tie score regulation game to determine the winner

Out of Bounds: When a player with the ball or the basketball itself is thrown outside the court boundaries and the clock stops

Pass: Throwing the basketball to a teammate

Penalty: A violation of the rules that results in a penalty for that team.

Personal Foul: A type of foul in which both the player and the team get charged with a foul

Pivot/Pivot Foot: When a player stops his or her dribble, the one foot that must be planted on the court while the other foot can be picked up and moved

Point Guard: A player who brings the ball up the court on offense and is usually a good dribbler, shooter, and passer

Points: Awards for scoring a basket. Most baskets are worth two points, a foul shot is one point, and a shot behind the three-point line is worth three points

Possession: When a team has the ball to shoot, dribble, or pass to other teammates

Press: When a team plays very tough aggressive defense at full court or half court, frequently "trapping" the ball (placing two men on the ball handler)

Pump Fake: When a player pretends to take a shot but passes, dribbles or shoots the basketball from a different area of the court

Quarter: The four segments that a timed basketball game is split into. The standard high school quarter is eight minutes; the NBA quarter is twelve minutes. College basketball is divided into two halves of twenty minutes each.

Rebound: When players try to get possession of the basketball after a shot has been taken

Referee: A person who makes decisions about rules, conduct, and guidelines during the game. There are typically two to three referees on the court at each game.

Rim: Round part of the basket that holds the net and is connected to the backboard

Three-Second Lane: An area on the court between the foul line and the baseline where an offensive player cannot "hang out" for more than three seconds

Turnover: An offensive mistake (for example "walking") that gives possession of the ball to the other team

Violation: A breaking of a basketball rule

Walking (or Traveling): A rules violation where a player who is not dribbling takes extra steps with the ball

Weak Side: The side of the court away from where the basketball is

Zone Defense: When a player defends an area on the court rather than a specific player (man-to-man)

Customizing Bball basics for Your Basketball Program

Anyone who is heading a basketball program should be most interested in the unique customization feature of this book.

- *How many kids can say that their picture is in a published basketball book?*

- *How many programs can boast that their program is highlighted in a published book?*

- *Think of the marketing potential. Such a customized book will help you with recruiting, publicity, community awareness, etc.*

I have designed Bball basics with this unique feature: You can customize and reproduce this book with your players' pictures substituted for the pictures in this book.

You as coaches, administrators, principals, camp directors, youth organizations leaders, parents, etc. can make this happen easily and have fun while doing it at a reasonable cost. Whether it's for an individual or a whole team, this customized book is the perfect keepsake gift during holiday times and other memorable occasions.

Trophies are nice, but why not award your coaches and players with this basic basketball book containing their pictures inside? What a great way of publicizing your program while producing a memento for years to come! The kids will treasure this keepsake forever.

In addition to pictures of your players, you can further personalize the contents of "your" version of **Bball basics** by adding a page at the beginning of the book describing you and your program (with pictures).

Think of the book as a template that can be customized for your use and is meaningful to kids since they're a part of it.

The procedure is simple. I will provide you with instructions for taking the pictures (following the layout in my book, for example, picture # 10, **Triple-threat position**, page 24).

You send (upload) your pictures to me, and I'll substitute your pictures for mine, and publish the book—at a very reasonable price.

The process for customizing to reflect your program is simple.

There are 73 pictures of children demonstrating the various basketball topics covered in the book. You may substitute all or just some of the pictures. If you have multiple programs, you can substitute pictures by

10: Triple-Threat Position   # 10: Triple-Threat Position

chapters in the book—each program doing a different chapter.

If you are interested in learning more about this unique option, see my website, **bballbasics.net,** or just e-mail me your cell number at **bballbasics@aol.com** and I'll call you to discuss further.

ACKNOWLEDGEMENTS

Bball basics is dedicated to every coach who, after losing a close one, went home and kicked the dog—figuratively, of course.

There are thousands of us out there coaching in high schools, elementary schools, community centers and on the basic playground. We work so hard for peanuts, volunteering a ton of extra hours to benefit the team while enduring and absorbing the scrutiny and criticism from "Monday morning" coaches, parents and game spectators.

And, a very special pat on the back to all those coaches of non-winning teams. You know it as well as I do—it is much more difficult to coach a team that has little hope of winning a playoff berth than one that is assured of making it. To teach a losing team to keep their heads up, play hard, and play with pride is a tremendous feat. Your effort and dedication to the kids does not go unnoticed. I salute you!

Only coaches can understand the overwhelming feelings of joy and accomplishment when their team finally executes a fast break as practiced, or when a key shot is made by a bench warmer who followed the shooting form you taught him. Nothing can match the exhilaration and pride for a job well done exhibited by players and coaches alike—that's why we play the game of basketball!

Bball basics was originally conceived as a rough handbook for my campers to take home to review and reinforce what they learned about playing the game of basketball at summer camp. Instrumental in its development was Head Coach Jeff "Listen up" Silverberg.

I would also like to thank my dear friends and fellow coaches who helped me fine-tune the material in this book, specifically: Ushie Selevan, Dr. Robert Greenblum and Stephanie Amos.

In addition, **Bball basics** could not have been completed without the tremendous photographic contribution of Dr. Jeff Kuritzky. Doctor Jeff sacrificed countless hours from his busy schedule to take most of the pictures that appear in *Bball basics*. Another photographer, Ari Levine, was a major help assisting with the taking of pictures at a moment's notice. Thanks to another friend, Morty Rosner, who assisted in the review and editing of this work. For their editorial and design review, I am also indebted to Emily R. Coleman, my friend and neighbor and my fellow teachers Tom Feigelson and Janet Chertkoff. Janet was a significant contributor to both the editorial and the content presentations of this book.

Thanks to my children and their spouses Ilana and Jeffrey, Debbie and Mordechai, and Daniella and Daniel for their constant support in all that I do. Their assistance in the editing and design stages was invaluable in seeing this book to fruition.

Of course, a special salute to my loving wife, Ruby. She is a paradigm for all those who endure their spouse's or partner's long coaching hours away from home whether it is for practice or a game. Ruby's enthusiasm and continuing support serve as a role model for all the better halves out there who tolerate the lives we coaches lead. Ultimately, her keen sense of understanding and sensitivity after every game, win or lose, was always appreciated.

120

Ruby and my children have always been my silent strength enabling me to ride with the highs and lows of coaching this great game.

And, thanks to the Township of Teaneck, New Jersey, specifically the Recreation Department for its support and cooperation regarding the various photo shoots.

Many others contributed in various ways to make this book happen. Thanks to Tzvika Poleyeff, Leor Rapps, Zvi Wolpoe, Eitan Selevan, Noam Kuritzky, Susan Herriot, and all the kids who participated in the photo shoots: Teji, Seti, Dennis, Darius, Khari W., Khari H., Naija, Amir, Hannah, Faith, Zach, Justin, Aden, Ben, Sammy, Solo, Sara, Menucha, Goldie, Lili, Rafi, Avi, Dovid, Aryeh, Eliana, Ilan, Aderet, Shira, Ora, and Max.

I must also mention my dear friends who had to listen to me talking about the book every chance I got: Milt, Ed, Lenny, Zvi, Robert, Paul, and David.

And, finally—may he rest in peace—to **Storm**, my English bulldog, who was the greatest mascot any team can have.

As you know, bulldogs generally do not bark. However, people came from far and wide to observe a phenomenon and to hear the unusual. Storm had the uncanny ability to bark when the opposing team shot a foul shot—but was quiet when his team attempted free throws. I often spoke to Storm about his lack of sportsmanship and disruptive conduct. He simply breathed heavily and slobbered a bit—I got the message!

INDEX: Where to find what in Bball basics

ABOUT THE AUTHOR

Bobby Kaplan has been coaching elementary, middle and high school students, both boys and girls, for over forty years.

His teams have played in and won numerous championships before scheduled New York Knick games at the famous Madison Square Garden arena and before New Jersey Net games at the renowned Continental Arena (now the Izod Center).

Coach K, as he is affectionately known, also owned and directed the Israel Basketball Academy (IBA) summer camp—both in Israel and in New York State for thirteen years. Bobby has coached more than twelve hundred games, played high school and college ball, and continues to coach both boys' and girls' varsity high school teams.

The author in the old, old days...nice form

"Give respect and you will receive respect" —Bobby Kaplan